GLADSTONE

Patricia Tweedie
Series editor: Christopher Culpin

LONGMAN

CONTENTS

Part 1   Telling the story   3

Part 2

1 From stern unbending Tory to leader of the Liberals   21

2 Gladstonian Liberalism   43

3 Gladstonian Liberalism in practice   60

4 Gladstone's foreign policy   77

5 Gladstone and Ireland   96

6 Gladstone's legacy   117

Further reading   126

Index   127

TELLING THE STORY

Family background and early life 1809–21

When Gladstone's background is described as 'middle class', it can give students today a misleading impression. It is true that the future Prime Minister did not have an aristocratic background or a title, but his father, though beginning his career as a corn merchant, became one of the wealthiest men in the country. William Ewart Gladstone was born on 29 December 1809, the fourth son and fifth child of John Gladstone and his wife, Anne. Neither parent was young – his father 45 and his mother 38. John Gladstone, a self-made man who had already accumulated a fortune of some £7 million in today's money, was almost totally occupied pursuing his many business and political interests and his wife had a full-time occupation as an invalid.

Gladstone's birthplace in Liverpool was a gracious Georgian house on four floors with a spacious drawing room, a dining room, a library, wine cellars and a bathroom. By 1811 John Gladstone decided it was no longer appropriate for his wealth and status. He began building himself a much grander house, outside Liverpool, but within a quarter of a mile of the sea. This was to all intents and purposes a 'statel home', set in grounds of 100 acres (40 hectares), with ornamental pond and gardens, with apricots, peaches and pineapples in glasshouses, with its own estate of a farm, a village of cottages, a church and a school. In many ways it was an idyllic place to spend a childhood, but young William was very much left to his own devices, especially when his older brothers were away at school. Apart from the family servants, he had no contact with the mass of humanity. The working class seem to have been regarded as a separate species. The children were taught to be charitable and in their personal accounts there were payments recorded 'to a poor little girl', 'to a poor Irish man', 'to a poor woman'.

As a supporter of George Canning, one of the MPs for Liverpool from 1812, John Gladstone began to have his own political ambitions, but found that though money could buy a seat in parliament, it could not guarantee a successful career there. Conscious of his own educational limitations, having left school at 13 with only the basics of literacy, he was determined to buy for his sons the kind of education that would achieve political success. Hence William followed his brothers to Eton, for this was where Canning had gone.

School and university 1821–31

Before he went to Eton when he was nearly 12, there were two quite distinct and conflicting influences on Gladstone at home. From his father he learned that it was his duty to work, to strive and to succeed in *this* life. From his mother on the other hand, whose religious beliefs were fanatical, he was taught that he must submit to God's will, that all men were sinners, that he must account to God for all his thoughts and deeds and he must prepare himself for the *next* life. Compared with meeting parental expectations, Eton was easy, despite the famous flogging headmaster who boasted of having beaten 80 boys in a day. The curriculum was very narrow, scarcely more than Latin and Greek, but with his retentive memory and attention to detail Gladstone was exceptionally good at these. He learned to debate (and found that he was very good at this too), he edited the school magazine and began his lifelong habit of voracious reading and noting down all the books he read in his journal. At this time he particularly enjoyed the novels of Sir Walter Scott. He read works on modern British history and each day he read the Bible as he had been taught to do at home. Science played no part in his studies or his reading and he was never to be interested in any of the sciences. Though a serious student, he must have had some fun at Eton – his nickname was 'Mr Tipple'.

From October 1828 Gladstone continued his studies at Oxford University. His father chose Christ Church because that was where Lord Liverpool, George Canning and Robert Peel had been. He studied more Greek and Latin, but also some theology and mathematics. He was elected President of the Oxford Union; he made speeches against Roman Catholic Emancipation and the Reform Bill. Gladstone excelled academically and gained two first-class degrees but perhaps more importantly, he made the right friends. Amongst them was Lord Lincoln, son of the Duke of Newcastle who had several parliamentary boroughs in his pocket.

Figure 1 Engraving of Gladstone as a young man

Member of parliament

Gladstone was first elected for parliament as a Conservative in December 1832, the first election following the Great Reform Act. He accepted the Duke of Newcastle's offer of a seat at Newark, an old pocket borough whose boundaries had not been changed. The borough was not completely in the Duke's pocket however: in 1831 a Whig had topped the poll despite the Duke of Newcastle evicting 40 tenants for failing to vote as he had instructed. It was estimated that he controlled about 700 votes and as there were now 1,600 voters compared with a mere 500 before the Great Reform Act, Gladstone had to do some canvassing. As well as delivering an election address he was expected 'to kiss the daughters. This latter was for me a rather novel occupation ... I fancy that my performances were considered to be rather sparing ...' He also had to answer some difficult questions on slavery. Among his father's many business enterprises were sugar plantations in the West Indies run on slave labour. When a slave uprising in 1823 was brutally suppressed John Gladstone became infamous. He became even more so after writing pamphlets defending the practice and attacking abolitionists. His son admitted he was 'unable to see the difficulties of emancipation ... in so strong a light as my father does'.

There were three candidates for two seats and Gladstone came top of the poll with 887 votes, almost a hundred more than the next candidate. The cost of his campaign was shared by his father and the Duke of Newcastle. Gladstone was shocked to find it amounted to over £2,000, more than twice the amount anticipated.

Travels and marriage

After leaving Oxford, Gladstone undertook a 'grand tour' of Europe with his 25-year-old brother, John Neilson. It had long been the custom for aristocratic young men to complete their education by visiting the chief cities of Europe. In paying for such a trip for his sons, John Gladstone was obviously hoping, once again, to buy his way into the upper classes. The brothers spent most of their time in the Italian peninsula, travelling as far south as Naples and returning home via Austria, Switzerland and steamboat down the Rhine. For Gladstone this was to be the first of many visits to Europe. He was a real tourist, an avid sightseer of both buildings and landscapes. At the age of 79 he went up the Eiffel Tower. Unlike his father, who as a young man had spent a year travelling the United States (1790–91), Gladstone did not venture beyond Europe, though he had many invitations to do so.

It was on another such visit to Europe (1838–39) that Gladstone met his future wife, Catherine Glynne. Gladstone had already attempted two courtships unsuccessfully. While he had been undoubtedly awkward and pompous, it is likely that both the young ladies were somewhat empty-headed and unsuitable matches. This time he proposed by moonlight in the Colosseum and was accepted in due course. There was a double wedding on 29 July 1839 at Hawarden Castle, Catherine's family home. Her younger sister, Mary, married Lord George Lyttleton.

Figure 2 Catherine Gladstone (née Glynne), painted by F. R. Say in 1840

Something of the scale of the celebrations can be gathered from the report in the local paper which described a wedding procession of 12 carriages with no less than four bands, followed by a dance for the villagers and by fireworks. Catherine brought her husband £8,666 on marriage and this, together with an increased allowance from his father, meant that Gladstone never needed to worry about money or concern himself with earning a living.

Catherine proved to be an ideal wife for Gladstone. She was totally unlike the females in his own immediate family, being full of health and vitality and not obsessed with religion. Their characters seemed to be complementary: whereas he was methodical and organised to the highest degree, accounting for practically every minute of his time, she was untidy and unpunctual; where he was serious, and forever examining his motives and conscience, she was vivacious and impulsive. Though she always gave him uncritical support in his political career, she was no doormat and had a wide range of interests of her own. It is interesting that, despite his wealth and now the aristocratic connections his father had hoped for, Gladstone still regarded himself as middle class. In 1843 he said: 'I ... with the family of which I am a member, still claim to belong to that middle class.'

Disciple of Peel

Gladstone began his career in the House of Commons as one of only 160 Tories under the leadership of Sir Robert Peel who was to become his role model and mentor. His first votes were in a typically Tory direction: for Irish coercion; against the admission of Jews to parliament and dissenters to universities; for the Corn Laws and Ashley's Factory Bill (see Chapter 1).

Apart from slavery, Gladstone spoke in 1833 against reform of the Church of Ireland. The proposal was to abolish ten bishoprics and use the superfluous revenues for other (lay) purposes. Gladstone argued that the State needed an established Church as its guide to divine truth and that Church revenues should not be used for lay purposes. He even voiced the opinion that the Bill endangered the union of England and Ireland. Religion was his main concern and interest at this time and by 1838 he had written his first book, published in two weighty volumes: *The State in its Relations with the Church*. It was really a defence of the role of the State Church which was under attack at this time from many quarters. According to Gladstone, the State had a duty to maintain the established Church as the repository of Divine Truth, against all other faiths which were in error. His ideas were not popular, after all there were large numbers of Radicals, Nonconformists, Roman Catholics, Jews and freethinkers in the country. The following year he opposed an increase in the government grant for education because he believed it should be exclusively for Anglican institutions.

Gladstone's opportunity for a sustained period in office came in 1841 when the Conservatives won the general election with a majority of

80. He was again returned as MP for Newark. One of the election issues was the unpopularity of the New Poor Law and Gladstone followed Peel in supporting the *principle* of the system while criticising the harshness of the régime in practice. At the Board of Trade he was able to demonstrate a formidable knowledge of commerce and finance, together with an outstanding administrative ability and attention to detail. His Railway Act in 1844, with the beginning of cheap travel for the poorer classes, brought him widespread popularity.

This period in office was cut short by Gladstone's resignation from the government over Peel's determination to increase the government grant to Maynooth College, the Irish institution for training Roman Catholic priests. Though Gladstone had come some distance from his intransigent position of 1838, he decided that in the interests of consistency, he must resign, though he later voted for the increase. Neither colleagues nor opponents could understand his motives. After Gladstone's resignation speech Cobden said: 'I know no more why he left the government than before he began.' Disraeli thought his career must be finished.

In the summer of 1845 Gladstone felt obliged to go to Baden-Baden where his sister had taken an overdose. An intelligent and good-looking woman, Helen had been kept at home to look after her invalid mother. By the time Anne Gladstone died in 1835 John Gladstone had returned to his Scottish roots and bought the large estate and gothic castle of Fasque in a beautiful but remote area between Dundee and Aberdeen, which he believed more appropriate to his vastly increased wealth. Unfortunately, Helen was completely isolated here and, without a role in life, turned to drink and drugs. Gladstone could never see why she needed to escape and regarded her behaviour only as a scandal bringing the family into disrepute.

When he returned to England late in 1845, the country was in the midst of the Corn Law crisis. There was news of famine in Ireland and fear of disorder. Peel offered Gladstone the position of Colonial Secretary. According to the law at the time, on accepting an office under the crown a new minister was obliged to seek re-election to parliament. Gladstone knew he could not stand again at Newark for the Duke of Newcastle was fiercely protectionist, but he was unable immediately to find a suitable constituency. Thus he was out of the Commons throughout the excitement of the Repeal of the Corn Laws.

Gladstone did not return to parliament until the following year when he became one of the two MPs for Oxford University, a seat he was to keep for 18 years. He followed Peel into the political wilderness but despite his admiration for his leader, he was both puzzled and frustrated by his distancing himself from political parties at this time: 'It might have been in his power to make some provision for the holding together, or for the reconstruction of that great party which he has reared ... But although that party was the great work of so many

Figure 3 William Gladstone, circa 1853–54

years of his matured life, his thought seemed simply to be, "It has fallen, there let it be".' Peel died in 1850 quite content in his 'elder statesman' role.

Family and private life

By 1850 Gladstone was well established as a family man. There were to be eight children in all – four boys and four girls – one of whom, Jessy, died in this year, aged four. Gladstone was much addicted to deathbed scenes, sitting down immediately to describe every part of the event in the utmost detail, but this was not untypical in Victorian times. Certainly unusual was Gladstone's obsession with saving prostitutes. He called it 'rescue work' and it began in a serious and systematic way in the 1850s when, following late-night sittings in the Commons, Gladstone would walk the streets of London, seeking out prostitutes whom he could then lecture on the evil of their ways. Once he had started this practice there was clearly a strong element of compulsion. He knew he was putting himself in temptation's way, but could not stop. To what extent his meetings with prostitutes went beyond mere talking it is impossible to know. Certainly he was only concerned with saving the souls of the young and beautiful. Not long before his death he told his son Stephen, then Rector of Hawarden, that he had never 'been guilty of the act which is known as that of infidelity to the marriage bed'. This was a rather obscure form of words, even for Gladstone, and might imply that he had been guilty of infidelity in other ways short of full sexual intercourse. On the other hand, he made no secret of his 'night walking' and he went straight to the police when there was a blackmail attempt in 1853. Quite what Catherine thought of her husband's unusual hobby, we do not know, but he does not seem to have kept it a secret from her, for we read in his diary of particular cases which he 'discussed with C' and sometimes he took prostitutes home. Several of Gladstone's political colleagues were worried for him, especially as he became a more and more important political figure, but he did not change his ways until he was in his seventies.

In many other ways, Gladstone seems to have led a life typical of a wealthy Victorian family man, except that he found time to do far more. As well as long hours in the Commons and on political work, he kept up an enormous correspondence, regularly writing 20 long letters by hand every day. There was usually some author whose work he was translating from the original Latin, Greek or Italian, and of course there was his enormous reading. He claimed to have read over 20,000 books in the course of his life. Since most of them still exist, full of annotations in his handwriting, in St Deiniol's, the library he founded at Harwarden, there is no reason to dispute his claim. Gladstone published numerous articles, reviews and pamphlets. Of course, whether in London, at Hawarden or on holiday, there was always a small army of servants to cater for the family's every need.

Gladstone always made time for lengthy holidays. He taught his children to ride and he played cricket with them. Particularly popular with the Gladstone family was the coast of north Wales where they swam in the sea and walked. This and climbing were Gladstone's favourite forms of exercise. At the age of 75 he climbed the highest peak in the Cairngorms. His sons became expert mountaineers, conquering among other peaks, the Eiger and the Jungfrau. Gladstone always walked the eight miles from Chester Station to Hawarden and when visiting his Lyttleton in-laws, walked the 12 miles from Birmingham Station to Hagley, their estate in Worcestershire. This doubtless helped to keep him fit, for though his diaries are full of references to the state of his bowels and minor stomach upsets, he was actually very fit and had immense stamina.

National statesman 1852–68

In the years following Peel's death, Gladstone became established as the leader of the Peelites and came to prominence as a reforming Chancellor of the Exchequer. As the possibility of a reconciliation with the Conservatives receded, Gladstone came to see that his future lay with the Liberals. In 1859, despite his dislike of him, he accepted the post of Chancellor in Palmerston's second ministry. Gladstone became widely popular through his public speaking around the country as well as his policies which gained general approval (see Chapter 1).

By the time of Palmerston's death in 1865, the demand for reform in the country was becoming difficult to resist. Russell, the new Prime Minister, hoped to repeat the success he had achieved in drafting the 1832 Reform Bill. The need to retain Radical support and his age (he was now 73) encouraged him to do this sooner, rather than later.

Figure 4 Gladstone in 1859, wearing 'broughams' – checked trousers named after Henry Brougham, with whom he was friendly in the 1850s

Gladstone's view was that reform should be cautious but he could see clear advantages of giving the vote to the more prosperous working men who seemed to appreciate his speeches so much. There were those in the party who wished to go much further, but not even John Bright advocated giving the vote to *all* the working class. Gladstone introduced the Reform Bill in the Commons on 12 March 1866, proposing to give the vote to householders in the boroughs paying at least £7 per year in rent and those in the counties paying at least £14. In the second reading debate Disraeli taunted Gladstone by recalling his speech to the Oxford Union in 1831 when he had been so vehemently against reform.

Gladstone summed up his argument for reform when he said: 'I believe that the composition of the House might be greatly improved and that the increased representation of the working classes would supply us more largely with the description of Members whom we want, who would look not to the interests of classes, but to the "public interest".' The opposition of the Liberal 'Adullamites', or cavemen, ensured the Reform Bill's defeat. When the government resigned the Conservative leader, Derby, agreed to form a minority government and such was the agitation in the country by now that a reform bill was inevitable. Disraeli for his part thought it could bring the Conservative's popularity, strengthen his own position and keep the Liberals divided. Gladstone decided to take his family on holiday to Italy for four months.

Prime Minister 1868–74

Gladstone's first ministry was the occasion for far-reaching reforms in many areas of life. (For domestic reforms see Chapter 3; for Irish reforms see Chapter 5.) Foreign affairs played a small part in the business of the ministry (see Chapter 4).

After the Liberals' general election defeat in February 1874, Gladstone resigned as party leader. During Disraeli's ministry (1874–80) the Liberal leadership was shared by Granville in the Lords and Hartington in the Commons. Gladstone spent his first year out of office writing articles on Homer and a book about Roman Catholic doctrine. He could not abandon active politics for long, however. From time to time he returned to sit on the opposition front bench to criticise, for example, Disraeli's purchase of the Suez Canal shares and the government's financial policy. But it was Disraeli's foreign policy which really brought him out of retirement. In August 1876 Disraeli became the Earl of Beaconsfield, hence the term, 'Beaconsfieldism' used to describe his foreign policy. Gladstone opposed this, not just in the House of Commons, but by writing pamphlets and speaking all over the country, culminating in his great Midlothian Campaign (see Chapter 4).

Relations with the Queen

Queen Victoria's tirades against Gladstone are well known. In 1880, when she heard of the Liberal victory in the general election, she wrote to her secretary Sir Henry Ponsonby, 'she will sooner *abdicate* than send for or have any *communication* with *that half-mad fire-brand* who wd soon ruin everything & be a Dictator'. She sent first for Hartington and Granville to ask each of them to form a government and only when they declined did she, with very bad grace, send for Gladstone.

Relations between them were not always as bad as this. In fact, when Victoria's husband, Prince Albert, was alive they got on remarkably well. Gladstone and Albert had much in common, both were admirers of Peel, and Gladstone was a commissioner for Albert's pet project, the Great Exhibition. Albert was a great admirer of Gladstone's policies as Chancellor of the Exchequer: they often discussed financial policy and in April 1853 he wrote to Gladstone to congratulate him on his Budget. The Gladstone children were much the same age as the royal children and were frequently invited to balls and children's dances at the Palace and at Windsor. Catherine was on particularly good terms with the Queen. After Albert's death in 1862 Gladstone was certainly preferred to 'those two dreadful old men' (Palmerston and Russell).

Their relationship began to disintegrate during Gladstone's first ministry. Victoria was opposed to the government's Army reforms and objected to Gladstone's attempts to persuade her to appear in public again. 1871 was the peak year of the republican movement. There was much criticism of the cost of the monarchy. Sir George Trevelyan wrote a pamphlet *What Does She Do With It?* The Queen took exception to Gladstone trying to find some purposeful occupation for her eldest son and she particularly disliked the way he lectured her and sent her long memoranda, large parts of which she did not understand.

The real turning point came during Disraeli's premiership (1874–80) because Disraeli was prepared to flatter the Queen, to treat her as a woman and make her feel important. She was delighted with the title Empress of India: she began to identify herself with his Conservative policies. Perhaps the most fundamental problem was that the Queen was jealous of Gladstone. She greatly disliked his being 'the People's William' and when he was acclaimed by enormous crowds on his speaking tours round the country, she felt he had usurped her relationship with her people. This jealousy reached a climax in 1883 when, in Copenhagen, he was feted by many of the crowned heads of Europe.

Relations between the two became worse and worse. The Queen strongly disapproved of Gladstone's Irish policies and his foreign policies. When Gladstone finally resigned in 1894 he thought the Queen dismissed him with the 'same brevity' as in 'settling a tradesman's bill'.

Prime Minister again 1880–85

Gladstone found it more difficult than he expected to reverse Disraeli's policies. In two years at the Exchequer (as well as being Prime Minister) he reduced public expenditure and was able to abolish the malt tax to help agriculture but he could not reduce the income tax. Apart from the Corrupt and Illegal Practices Act (see page 125), the chief legislation was the Representation of the People Act 1884, which extended the vote to the rural working class so doubling the electorate, and the Redistribution of the Seats Act 1885, which corrected some serious anomalies in parliamentary representation and was a substantial move towards single member constituencies. (For Irish legislation see Chapter 5; for foreign policy see Chapter 4.)

Last years

Gladstone's last years were devoted to trying to implement Home Rule which by now he had decided was the solution to the Irish problem (see Chapter 5). When he finally resigned in 1894 it was in opposition to the proposed increase in the Navy estimates which he saw as taking part in the arms race. 'If I stood alone in the world on this question, I could not be moved: so strongly am I convinced that this large increase to the Navy will lead to disaster in Europe – *Europe* is my watchword.'

Gladstone's retirement, commencing at the age of nearly 85, was inevitably short. His eyesight was poor, despite a cataract operation, and he finally gave up his journal. He spent the winters in Cannes but returned to Hawarden to die in May 1898. The State funeral was in Westminster Abbey with no soldiers or military bands in sight. Against the Queen's wishes, the Prince of Wales and his son, the future George V, were pall bearers.

Key events

1809	Born in Liverpool
1821–7	At school at Eton
1828–31	At Oxford University
1831	Speech against Reform Bill at Oxford Union
1832	Elected Tory MP for Duke of Newcastle's pocket borough of Newark
1835	Under-Secretary for War and the Colonies in Peel's government (1834–35)
1838	First book published *The State in its Relations with the Church*
1839	Marriage to Catherine Glynne
1841	Vice President of the Board of Trade (from 1843, President) in Peel's government (1841–46)
1844	Railway Act
1845	Resignation from cabinet over Maynooth Grant
1846–52	Out of office
1850–51	Visit to Naples and publication of letter to Aberdeen
1852	Chancellor of the Exchequer in Aberdeen's Whig-Peelite government (1852–55)
1853	First budget
1855–9	Out of office
1859	Chancellor of the Exchequer in Palmerston's Liberal government (1859–65)
1860	Great Budget; Commercial (Cobden) Treaty with France
1861	Post Office Savings Act; repeal of paper duties
1862	First public speaking tour (Newcastle and the North)
1864	'Pale of the constitution' speech on electoral reform
1865	Death of Palmerston: leader of the party in the Commons
1866	Failure of Liberal Reform Bill and resignation of government
1867	Second Reform Act passed by minority Conservative government
1868–74	First ministry
1869	Dis-establishment of the Irish Church Act
1870	Elementary Education Act; Army reforms; civil service Reform; First Irish Land Act
1871	University Tests Act; Trade Union Act; Criminal Law Amendment Act; Army reforms
1872	Ballot Act; Licensing Act
1873	Defeat of Irish Universities Bill: unsuccessful resignation Chancellor of the Exchequer as well as Prime Minister Second Ashanti War; Judicature Act
1874	Defeat of Liberals: Disraeli Prime Minister of Conservative government
1875	Resignation of leadership of Liberal Party; announcement of retirement
1876	Campaign against Bulgarian atrocities
1879	Midlothian Campaign

1880–5	Second Ministry
1881	Second Irish Land Act; death of Disraeli
1882	Phoenix Park murders; Married Women's Property Act
1883	Corrupt and Illegal Practices Act
1884	Third Reform Act
1885	Death of Gordon; Redistribution of Seats Act; resignation as Prime Minister; conversion to Home Rule
1886	Third Ministry; First Home Rule Bill: electoral defeat
1891	Death of Parnell
1892–4	Fourth Ministry
1893	Second Home Rule Bill – defeated in Lords
1894	Resignation as Prime Minister and retirement
1898	Death

Gladstone's constituencies

1832–45	Newark
1847–65	Oxford University
1865–8	South Lancashire
1868–80	Greenwich
1880–95	Midlothian

Benjamin DISRAELI *1804–81*

(created Earl of Beaconsfield 1876)

As a son of a Jewish writer, and without wealth or a traditional upper-class education, Disraeli was always regarded as an outsider in politics. He entered the Commons in 1837 as a Tory. He opposed Peel over free trade in 1846 and as a Protectionist was only briefly in office during the 1850s and 1860s, though he was responsible for the Second Reform Act (1867). As Conservative Prime Minister (1874–80) his chief interests lay in foreign affairs and the empire, but his government was responsible for some important social reforms. He supplemented his income by writing successful novels.

John BRIGHT *1811–89*

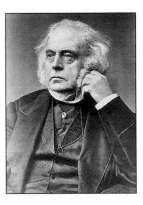

Born in Rochdale, he was the son of a textile manufacturer and entered his father's business on leaving school. A Quaker, he met Cobden in 1835 and after his wife's death in 1841 gave most of his time to the Anti-Corn Law League. He was MP for Durham (1843–47), Manchester (1847–57) and Birmingham (1857–89). He was also the first English Nonconformist to sit in cabinet and was President of the Board of Trade (1868–70). In 1884 he proposed a scheme to limit the power of the House of Lords and in 1886 opposed Home Rule.

Joseph CHAMBERLAIN *1836–1914*

Born in London but made his fortune as a screw manufacturer in Birmingham where, as Mayor (1873–76), he made many improvements to the city. He was MP for Birmingham (1876–86) and played a key role in making the National Liberation Federation an efficient party machine. He was President of the Board of Trade (1880–85) but split with Gladstone over Home Rule in 1886, becoming a Liberal Unionist. He subsequently joined the Conservatives, serving in Salisbury's government as Colonial Secretary (1895–1902).

Sir Robert PEEL *1788–1850*

Son of a wealthy cotton manufacturer, Peel was a
brilliant student at Harrow and Christ Church, Oxford. An
MP at 21, he became Chief Secretary for Ireland in
Liverpool's Tory government at 24. As Home Secretary he
introduced prison reforms and founded the Metropolitan
Police. In 1834, in a speech to his constituents at
Tamworth, he outlined a new philosophy for his party; as
Prime Minister (1841–46) he was responsible for a series of
Free Trade Budgets and introduced important
financial reforms, but he split the Conservative Party
twice, over Catholic Emancipation in 1829 and Repeal of
the Corn Laws in 1846.

Lord PALMERSTON *1784–1865*

As an Irish peer, Palmerston was able to sit in the
Commons. As a Tory MP he was Secretary at War
(1809–28) and his chief interest was always foreign
affairs. He joined the Whigs in 1829 and was twice
Foreign Secretary (1830–41 and 1846–51), gaining a
reputation for a vigorous, patriotic policy and blunt
speaking. After a spell as Home Secretary (1852–55), the
public clamoured for him to become Prime Minister
during the disasters of the Crimean War. As Prime
Minister (1855–8 and 1859–65), though he remained
popular, his foreign policy became less successful.

Queen VICTORIA *1819–1901*

Succeeding her uncle, William IV, in 1837, Victoria was
responsible for restoring the popularity of the monarchy
after the contempt in which the later Hanoverians had
been held. In 1840 she married her cousin, Albert, who
became her chief adviser until his death in 1861. Victoria
was then so distraught she became virtually a recluse,
and consequently unpopular, until Disraeli's flattery
brought her back into public life. Though a
constitutional monarch, she held strong views on most
political issues and expressed her prejudices forcibly to
her ministers.

PART TWO

CHAPTER ONE

FROM STERN UNBENDING TORY TO LEADER OF THE LIBERALS

Objectives
◢ To investigate and explain Gladstone's transition from Tory to Liberal
◢ To explain how he became leader of the Liberals.

The transition to Liberalism

A typical Tory?

The young man who, at 23, became one of the Tory MPs for the Duke of Newcastle's pocket borough of Newark in December 1832, would seem an unlikely candidate for future Liberal leadership.

It was Thomas Macaulay, reviewing Gladstone's first book, *The State in its Relations with the Church*, who described him as 'the rising hope of those stern and unbending Tories'. But there is evidence to suggest that Gladstone was never a typical Tory. While it is true that he had the traditional classical education of an aristocrat at Eton and Christ Church, Oxford – the college of Liverpool, Canning and Peel – he was the son of a merchant. Though a High Church Anglican, he had been brought up in an evangelical household where sin and retribution were the dominant beliefs. At Eton he had been taught the Whig view of history. At the Oxford Union, in May 1831, he spoke passionately against the Whig Reform Bill although only six months before he had moved and carried a motion of no confidence in the Tory government of the Duke of Wellington. Two months after speaking so forcibly against the Reform Bill, he was writing a pamphlet advocating a limited redistribution of seats, together with mild franchise and corrupt practices reform! In his election address Gladstone announced that 'it is a duty to endeavour by every means that labour may receive adequate remuneration; which, unhappily, among several classes of our fellow-countrymen, is not now the case' – an opinion very untypical of Tory MPs.

Once in the House of Commons, however, his maiden speech in June 1833 was against the Whigs' Slavery Abolition Bill. Gladstone's stance on slavery was heavily influenced by his father, whose plantations in Demerara and Jamaica were worked by slaves. Both Gladstone and his brother felt obliged to defend their father's interests, though Gladstone's speech concentrated on the *terms* of emancipation rather than the principle. He said the Bill made no provision to integrate the slaves into colonial society and he favoured delay until the slaves had become Christians. This speech lasted 50 minutes, was well received in the House and noticed by the senior Tory politician, Robert Peel, who perhaps already recognised Gladstone as a man for future promotion. Thus Gladstone set out on his parliamentary career in the Tory fold though there were already some signs of the differences to come.

Gladstone's transition to Liberalism was a gradual one, although a number of stages can be identified. Several factors served to push Gladstone away from the Tories and towards Liberalism. Perhaps surprisingly, since he was the Tory party leader, the first of these influences was Peel.

The influence of Peel

Peel had a most important influence on Gladstone's political career, one which was to last all his life. The two men had much in common despite being separated by a generation. Both were the sons of exceptionally wealthy men who had made fortunes in the appalling conditions of the industrial revolution: among the 15,000 workers employed by Robert Peel senior in his calico printing factories in Lancashire were many exhausted and malnourished children. Both men transferred to their sons the high political ambitions they themselves were unable to fulfil. Both Peel and Gladstone were first-generation public school and university students, though Peel went to Harrow. Both attended the same Oxford college, Christ Church, where each gained a double first and both became MPs within a year of leaving university.

Years later, in the early 1880s, Gladstone wrote: 'I was trained in a Conservative school ... of Economy, Peace, Sound and strict finance ... Maintenance of the sound traditions of Parliament and of administration.' These were lessons learned from Peel who recognised Gladstone's ability early. In December 1834, following the King's dismissal of Melbourne's reforming Whig ministry, Peel, as the new Prime Minister, asked Gladstone to be sixth Lord of the Treasury. After the 1835 general election he became Under-Secretary for the Colonies. Since his senior at the Colonial Office, the EARL OF ABERDEEN, sat in the Lords, Gladstone had to speak for the department in the Commons. It was a considerable promotion for someone just 25 years old.

Gladstone formed a lasting regard for Aberdeen. After Peel, Aberdeen was the second most important influence in forming his political views. Aberdeen was a pacifist: he had seen the brutality of war at first hand and believed that nothing could justify it. He was a friend of other European statesmen such as Metternich and was able to see foreign affairs from a more European, less insular and purely nationalist point of view than was often the case at this time. Gladstone adopted these ideas and honed them into his own version of international morality. Unfortunately, his association with Aberdeen at this time was short, for at the beginning of April 1835 Peel's government fell and Gladstone was out of office for the next six years. Even in this short time, however, he had impressed civil servants with his industry and organisation.

Profile GEORGE HAMILTON-GORDON, 4TH EARL OF ABERDEEN (1784–1860)

An orphan at 11, came under the patronage of Pitt; educated at Harrow and St John's College, Cambridge; wife died young of tuberculosis, also three daughters under 21; helped to bring Austria into coalition against Napoleon in 1813 while ambassador; Foreign Secretary (1828–30; 1841–46); Secretary for War and the Colonies (1834–35); Prime Minister (1852–55), resigned after censure over Crimean War.

Out of office, Gladstone pursued his political career by sitting on parliamentary committees and making speeches both inside the House of Commons and out. Many of these still had a strong Tory flavour. For example, in 1838 he spoke against the proposal to reduce the apprenticeship period of the former slaves. This was clearly out of filial duty and he agonised over 'pleading the cause of injustice' – another sign that he was moving towards a more liberal position.

It was also in 1838 that Gladstone published his first book, mentioned in Part 1, page 8. It was hastily written in two months – a work remarkable both for its intolerance and the obscurity of its prose. Briefly, its thesis was that the State must have a national church (i.e. the Church of England), its doctrines amounted to The Truth, all other religious doctrines were in error and believers of other Churches should be denied civil rights. This was an extreme position even for a Tory to take. Peel is said to have thrown the book on the floor in disgust and said, 'that young man will ruin a fine career if he writes such books as these'.

At the same time as Gladstone held these extreme views about Church and State, he seemed to be moving towards a more liberal position in foreign affairs. In 1840, in the debates on the Opium War against China, he was heavily critical of Palmerston's policy of aggression, condemning both the war and the opium trade. He spoke of 'our national iniquity against China' and 'this infamous and atrocious traffic'. Perhaps it would be unwise, however, to place too much emphasis on this speech as evidence of Gladstone's approaching liberalism: it could be that he had special concerns about the opium trade because of the drug addiction of his sister Helen.

Gladstone returned to office in August 1841 when Peel, on becoming Prime Minister of a majority Conservative government, appointed him Vice President of the Board of Trade under the EARL OF RIPON. Gladstone was both indignant and disappointed with this post: 'the science of politics deals with the government of men, but I am set to govern packages'. Membership of Peel's meetings to plan tactics during the summer, together with his own estimate of his abilities, had led him to expect a cabinet post. But secondly, he claimed to have neither knowledge nor interest in this area of government: 'I was totally ignorant both of political economy and the commerce of the country.' Nevertheless, he set about mastering his brief with characteristic thoroughness. Since Ripon sat in the Lords, Gladstone had to speak for the department in the Commons; Ripon, perhaps bored with a post he had first held 25 years ago, also left most of the work to his eager and ambitious lieutenant.

Free trade

It was his work at the Board of Trade that led Gladstone to his belief in free trade as the means to national prosperity. Until this time his economic views had been those of a moderate Tory, a follower of WILLIAM HUSKISSON: that is, he favoured mild tariff reforms. Once in office he

Profiles
FREDERICK JOHN ROBINSON, CREATED VISCOUNT GODERICH 1827, EARL OF RIPON 1833 (1782–1859)

Educated Harrow and Cambridge; MP, 1806; President of the Board of Trade (1816–23); Chancellor of the Exchequer (1823–27) (nicknamed 'Prosperity Robinson' by Cobbett); became Prime Minister August 1827 on the death of Canning but resigned January 1828 unable to control the fractious and divided cabinet; President of the Board of Trade again (1841–43); President of the Board of Control (1843–46).

WILLIAM HUSKISSON (1770–1830)

Lived in France 1783–92 and witnessed events of the French Revolution at first hand; MP for Liverpool, 1796; President of the Board of Trade in Tory ministries of Liverpool and Canning (1823–28); able financier, began policy of reducing tariffs; Secretary for War and the Colonies under Goderich and Wellington (1827–28); resigned 1828; first casualty of the railway age, run down by a train at the official opening of the Manchester to Liverpool line.

RICHARD COBDEN (1804–65)

Born in Midhurst, Sussex into a farming family but after working as a clerk in London set up a calico printing business in Manchester; founder and leading member of Anti-Corn Law League, 1839, along with John Bright. MP for Stockport (1841–47), West Riding of Yorkshire (1847–57), Rochdale (1859–65): lost his seat in 1857 because opposition to the Crimean War had made him highly unpopular, although when his business was almost ruined in 1845, £80,000 was collected for him by public subscription; refused to serve as President of the Board of Trade under Palmerston in 1859 because he had always opposed his jingoistic foreign policy.

rapidly mastered the detail of the multiplicity of complex tariffs that applied to Britain's international trade. He soon came to the conclusion that a reduction in tariffs would lead to an increase in trade and thence to an increase in revenues rather than a decrease as many thought. Gladstone came to this position through practical experience rather than economic theory. He had no sympathy with RICHARD COBDEN and the Anti-Corn Law League at this time. As far as he was concerned, ending the Corn Law was merely part of a general move towards freer trade and cheaper food.

At the beginning of his ministry Peel's concerns were:
◢ to reduce the budget deficit bequeathed by the Whigs
◢ to revive trade and employment
◢ to legislate to control new developments (e.g. the railways).

The Board of Trade was to be the crucial department in carrying out these policies and it was Gladstone's work which formed the basis of Peel's great Budget of 1842 in which customs duties were reduced on 750 articles. Peel was certainly appreciative and wrote in fulsome praise to Gladstone's father: 'At no time in the annals of parliament has there been exhibited a more admirable combination of ability, extensive knowledge, temper and discretion.' The Home Secretary, Sir James Graham, also wrote to John Gladstone: 'I have no doubt he will rise to great eminence and give to your name an enduring place in the history of our country.'

Peel recognised Gladstone's ability when, in May 1843, he promoted him to President of the Board of Trade with a seat in the cabinet of 14 members. Gladstone's main concern now was the regulation of the railways which were spreading all over the land. There were, at this time, some 2,000 miles of track and the country was on the verge of 'railway mania': more than 3,000 would be opened in the next five years. Gladstone aimed to promote the interests of the consumer against those of the railway entrepreneurs.

1844 Railway Act
◢ A separate Railways Board was created with railway commissioners having powers of inspection and accident investigation.
◢ A new railway company's profits should not exceed 10% per annum.
◢ If rates exceeded 10% for three consecutive years, the Board of Trade could force the rates down or the line could be purchased by the State.
◢ These powers were to come into effect after 21 years; a specific act of parliament would be required for each railway company.
◢ All railway companies must run a passenger service each weekday, with covered carriages, at a speed of at least 12 miles per hour, stopping at every station and costing a maximum of 1d per mile.

It was these statutory 'parliamentary trains', providing cheap travel, which first brought Gladstone to the notice of 'the people'. This was the beginning of his popularity and his becoming a national figure. The clauses of the Railway Act are interesting because they show just how far Gladstone was prepared to go in terms of State intervention: he was actually laying the foundations for the nationalisation of the railways.

The Repeal of the Corn Laws 1846

Gladstone's free trade credentials were confirmed by his support for Peel over the Repeal of the Corn Laws. Gladstone saw repeal in the context of the general removal of tariffs and the progress to freer trade. He had little sympathy with the ideas of Cobden and Bright and the Anti-Corn Law League. He would have agreed with Peel's words when he told his Tamworth constituents in 1847 that Repeal 'tended to fortify the established institutions of this country, to inspire confidence in the equity and benevolence of the legislature, to maintain the just authority of an hereditary nobility, and to discourage the desire for democratic change in the constitution of the House of Commons'. Unfortunately for Peel, Gladstone was unable to speak in his support in the House of Commons during the Corn Law crisis. Having recently (December 1845) accepted the office of Colonial Secretary in Peel's cabinet reshuffle, he was obliged to seek re-election and he knew he would not be acceptable now to his protectionist patron the Duke of Newcastle. Thus he was temporarily out of the Commons until he found another constituency and was unable to reply to Disraeli's invective. Once elected for Oxford University in the general election of late summer 1847, Gladstone joined the Peelites in the political wilderness, their position worsened by their leader's sudden death in 1850.

Visit to Italy

The next stage in Gladstone's progress towards Liberalism occurred as a result of his visit to Italy in 1850. The primary reason for the visit was apparently to have a holiday to restore the health of his wife and daughter Mary. Gladstone's self-imposed holiday task was to translate from the Italian the three volumes of Farini's *Lo Stato Romano*. Farini was a liberal and it was partly through reading his work that Gladstone became more interested in the affairs of Naples. The King of Naples had recently earned the title of 'King Bomba' through his ruthless bombardment of Sicilian towns following the 1848 revolutions. Thousands of political opponents had been thrown into jail and Gladstone visited one Baron Carlo Poerio, a former minister, now sentenced to 24 years in irons. He was absolutely appalled to see the conditions in the dungeons where political prisoners were held. In one prison he saw '16 prisoners confined in a room about 16 palms in length by 10 or 12 in breadth and 10 in height', permanently chained and without food other than that brought in by visitors. He was particularly incensed that the educated elite was being especially targeted: 'The class persecuted as a whole is ... the middle class ... but particularly in the upper part of the middle class which it may be said embraces the professions, the most cultivated and progressive part of the nation.'

Gladstone returned to London in February 1851 determined to do something. ('One grows wild at being able to do nothing.') He decided to enlist the help of Aberdeen as a former Conservative Foreign Secretary and a former ambassador to Austria, the country with the most influence over Naples. (Austrian soldiers had been responsible for restoring the tyrant King Ferdinand after the Napoleonic wars.) Aberdeen agreed to help and in due course wrote to the Austrian Chancellor, Schwartzenberg, who took a further seven weeks to reply. He pointed out the British ill treatment of prisoners in Ireland and even England (the name of a Chartist was invoked). Gladstone was infuriated by now and decided to publish his 'Letter to Aberdeen' as a pamphlet. It was here that he used his famous phrase describing the rule in Naples as 'the negation of God erected into a system of government'. Almost overnight, Gladstone outraged conservative opinion both at home and in Europe and found himself ranked with liberals and even revolutionaries. It was the first time that he appealed to public opinion, but the real significance of the 'Letters to Aberdeen' (for there was a second), was that they opened the way for him to work with Palmerston who took up the letters enthusiastically and had them distributed to British embassies in all the European capitals. While Gladstone may not yet have been ready to adopt the cause of Italian nationalism, this was a point of contact between himself and Palmerston, a further distancing of himself from the Conservatives and another step towards Liberalism.

Leader of the Peelites

When Gladstone returned from Italy Edward Stanley (soon to be the EARL OF DERBY), was trying to form a Conservative government. To do this, he needed the support of the Peelites and he offered Gladstone 'almost *any* office' if he would join his administration. Although Gladstone was very keen to resume government office, Stanley and the Protectionists intended restoring a small duty on corn and this was the deciding factor in Gladstone's refusal. Gladstone still claimed to be a Conservative and hoped that one day the party would be reunited, but he was not prepared to compromise his free trade principles. It is significant that Stanley made his approach to Gladstone. Perhaps he thought he was the Peelite most likely to be enticed back into the Conservative fold, but more likely, it was a recognition of Gladstone's standing as the leading Peelite in the House of Commons.

Profile EDWARD STANLEY, 14TH EARL OF DERBY (1799–1869)

Educated Eton and Christ Church, Oxford; as Lord Stanley he sat in Commons as a Whig MP (1820–35); member of Grey's Reform Ministry (1831–34); Secretary for War and Colonies under Peel (1841–45); resigned over protection; Prime Minister three times – for nine months in 1852, 17 months in 1858–59 and June 1866–Feb 1868 when he was responsible, with Disraeli, for the Second Reform Act.

Gladstone further established his liberal credentials a month later when he made a great speech against the Ecclesiastical Titles Bill. The Pope had decided to re-establish the Roman Catholic hierarchy in England, dividing the country into 12 dioceses each with a bishop, and a cardinal-archbishop at Westminster. This unleashed a wave of anti-papist hysteria across the country: effigies of the Pope and other leading Catholics were burnt on bonfires and in response to the public agitation, Russell introduced legislation to try to thwart the Pope's plans. Gladstone opposed the second reading of the Bill in a two and a half hour speech in which he argued for religious toleration. He wrote to his sister Helen: 'I am inflexibly opposed to all Bills against religious liberty.' Perhaps more important than demonstrating his liberalism, this greatly increased Gladstone's reputation as a star parliamentary performer: clearly he could be a great asset to whichever political party he chose to join.

Although, according to Gladstone, 'junction with the Liberals' was 'our least natural position' at this time, his return to the Conservative Party was looking increasingly unlikely. Meanwhile Russell's government limped to an end. Palmerston's dismissal at the insistence of Victoria and Albert proved fatal. Derby, again unable to persuade the Peelites to join him, formed a weak Conservative government which lasted from February to December 1852. The curious position of the Peelites is well illustrated here in their dilemma in deciding where to sit in the House of Commons. Since their split with the Protectionist Conservatives in 1846 they had continued to sit on their side of the House (i.e. on the opposition side). Having refused to serve with Derby, they could hardly now move with his Conservatives to the government side; yet if they stayed on the opposition benches, they would be on the same side as the Liberals. Gladstone's preference was to stay on the Conservative side, partly because he still regarded himself as a Conservative and partly because he hoped and expected that it would not be long before Derby accepted the inevitability of free trade. The Peelites, however, decided to sit with the Liberals and Gladstone stayed with them. This proximity to the Liberals was more than symbolic: it paved the way for the Peelites joining a coalition with them.

The general election of July 1852 produced no overall majority and so, although the Peelites were reduced to between 30 and 40 members, they had a disproportionate influence. They decided to give Derby's government a chance and waited to see what Disraeli produced in his budget. Gladstone had already told his wife that 'Disraeli could not have been worse placed than at the Exchequer'. He now found in his budget 'fundamental faults of principle which it is impossible to overlook' and he wrote that it was 'the least conservative budget I have ever known'. Disraeli made his final speech, which should have concluded the budget debate, amid a violent thunderstorm, punctuated by flashes of lightning and rolls of thunder. At the end, and quite without precedent for he had already spoken twice in the debate, Gladstone leapt to his feet (it was one o'clock in the morning) and made a devastating speech which demolished Disraeli's budget and with it, the government. After this it was clear there could be no reconciliation between the Peelites and the Conservatives, although Gladstone, even at this late stage, regarded himself as a Conservative, as he made clear in his speech:

If I vote against the government I vote in support of those Conservative principles which I thank God are common in a great degree to all parties in the British House of Commons, but of which I thought it was the peculiar pride and glory of the Conservative Party to be the champions and the leaders.

Gladstone's apparently impromptu speech also marked the real beginning of the duel between him and Disraeli. Although Gladstone had already decided that Disraeli was an adventurer and not to be trusted, their rivalry now took on a degree of personal animosity rare in English politics. Gladstone's speech, seen by some historians as a calculated bid for power, was an important contributory factor in leading to his becoming leader of the Liberal Party.

Chancellor of the Exchequer

Derby resigned and Aberdeen became Prime Minister of a Whig–Peelite coalition government. He appointed Gladstone Chancellor of the Exchequer, as the obvious person for the post since making that great speech a few days before. Gladstone was to prove the greatest Chancellor of the nineteenth century and he increased the importance of the post so that it became second only to the premiership. The success and the popularity he achieved were enormously important factors in bringing him to the leadership of the Liberal Party.

Gladstone's economic policy, unlike those of his predecessors, involved the long-term reconstruction of public finance, rather than short-term strategies. In making his first budget Gladstone's main problem was the income tax. This had been an unpopular tax ever since its first introduction by Pitt in 1799 to pay for the Napoleonic Wars, yet it was efficient and effective. Gladstone wanted to retain it because he needed its revenue to replace that which he would lose by his free trade measures. He solved his dilemma with great skill.

Gladstone introduced his first budget in the House of Commons on 18 April 1853 in a four-and-three-quarter hour speech, the longest he ever made. He proposed to:

◢ retain the income tax for seven more years

◢ extend it to Ireland

◢ lower the exemption rate from £150 to £100 (but to exclude life insurance premiums)

◢ levy the tax at 7*d* in the £ from 1853–55

at 6*d* in the £ from 1855–57

at 5*d* in the £ from 1857–60

when he said the tax would be abolished.

In addition:

◢ protective tariffs (customs duties) were removed from 123 partly manufactured articles and food, including fruit and dairy produce.

◢ duties on a further 133 wholly manufactured goods were reduced.

◢ excise duty on soap was abolished.

This first budget was a tremendous success. Russell described it as 'one of the most powerful financial speeches ever made'. Clarendon called it 'the most perfect financial statement ever heard within the walls of parliament for such it is allowed to be by friend and foe'. Gladstone had skilfully wrongfooted his opponents. Those against the income tax were placated: Gladstone agreed it was both a temptation to commit fraud and an unfair demand because it pressed too hard 'upon intelligence or skill, and not hard enough upon property' (there were the beginnings here of a distinction between earned and unearned income) and he promised its abolition in 1860. Those, like the Radicals, who approved of the tax, were pleased at its continuation. Gladstone also won support for his campaign to reduce government expenditure, although this was then very low anyway. (In 1853 it was just 8.6% of gross national product.)

The success of his budget meant considerable acclaim for Gladstone personally. Charles Greville, clerk to the Privy Council, said that Gladstone had 'given the country the assurance of a man equal to great political necessities and fit to lead parties and direct governments'. Aberdeen appreciated what it meant for his own government and told Gladstone: 'If the existence of my government shall be prolonged, it will be your work.' But what is so remarkable is that we can see in Gladstone's very first budget those fundamental principles which were to form the basis of all his financial measures throughout his career, namely:

- ◢ to expand free trade by reductions in tariffs, especially on consumer goods and foodstuffs in order to lower the cost of living;
- ◢ to spread taxation as equitably as possible;
- ◢ to reduce government expenditure as much as possible to allow for tax reductions;
- ◢ to make government services as economical and efficient as possible to give the tax payers best value for money;
- ◢ to encourage people to save.

Junction with the Liberals

The Aberdeen Coalition broke up in 1855, defeated on a censure motion prompted by the defeats in the Crimea (see Chapter 4). Palmerston eventually formed a Liberal government which included some Peelites, though Gladstone served for only two weeks. Agreement over Italy did not make sufficient common cause for Gladstone to work with Palmerston at this stage: Gladstone still felt great antipathy to his personality. No great issues of policy separated the Peelites from the Tories now that the latter had abandoned protectionism, as Gladstone recognised when he wrote in the *Quarterly Review* in 1856: 'The interval between the two parties has, by the practical solution of so many congested questions, been very greatly narrowed.' Indeed, on some questions Gladstone found it easier to work with the Conservatives but on others, such as the conduct of the war, finance and administrative reform, he found himself closer to the ideas of the Manchester School of Cobden and Bright. In common with them and other Radicals, Gladstone now found himself very unpopular because of his campaigning for peace negotiations to start rather than a more vigorous prosecution of the war and the punishment of Russia. The one group that Gladstone rarely found himself in sympathy with at this time was the Whigs: not only did he disagree with Palmerston's foreign policy, which he regarded as unprincipled, but he viewed his government's financial policy as misguided and its policy on divorce as immoral. In his opposition to Palmerston's war against China Gladstone found himself in the same division lobby as such an ill-assorted crew as Cobden, Derby, Disraeli and Russell.

Thus Gladstone was destined to spend some years in the political wilderness, but he felt the loss of office keenly. In 1856 he drew up a detailed programme of 21 financial measures which he intended to implement on his return to office. The following year he told his friend, Samuel Wilberforce: 'I greatly felt being turned out of office, I saw great things to do. I longed to do them. I am losing the best years of my life out of my natural service . . .' In his diary he commented: 'He must be a very bad minister indeed, who does not do ten times the good to the country when he is in office, that he would do when he is out of it.' The 1857 general election saw the Peelites further reduced in numbers and Gladstone then offending them by his opposition to the government's Divorce Bill. Yet he still saw himself as first and foremost a Peelite. He told the editor of the *Quarterly Review*:

There is a policy going a-begging; the general policy that Sir Robert Peel in 1841 took office to support – the policy of peace abroad, of economy, of financial equilibrium, of steady resistance to abuses, and promotion of practical improvements at home, with a disinclination to questions of reform gratuitously raised.

It seemed that Gladstone just could not decide which party he should join in order to implement these policies. He must have known that when he did decide his decision would have to be final.

Following Palmerston's fall in 1858, Derby again asked Gladstone to join the minority government he was trying to form. The Conservatives were eager to have Gladstone in the cabinet but had no room for other Peelites. In addition, and perhaps more important as far as Gladstone was concerned, Disraeli was by now clearly the leading Conservative in the Commons and he was not prepared to work with him. As his brother Robertson, now Mayor of Liverpool, wrote: 'No one, who knows you, if he ever thinks, can suppose that you would coalesce with D'Israeli: when *you* join with another, that move, we know, will have some sort of principle, at least, to boast of.' Possibly Gladstone was influenced by a letter from John Bright, advising him:

If you join Lord Derby, you link your fortunes with a constant minority which is every day lessening in numbers and power . . . Will you unite yourself with what must be, from the beginning, an inevitable failure? . . . If you remain on our side of the House . . . I know nothing that can prevent your being Prime Minister ... I think I am not mistaken in the opinion I have formed of the direction in which your views have for some years been tending.

Thus Gladstone rejected government office under Derby, but he proceeded to accept a rather strange commission to go to the Ionian Islands as Lord High Commissioner Extraordinary. This provoked the exasperated comment from Sidney Herbert: 'He really is not safe to go out of Lord Aberdeen's room. It is heartbreaking to see him throwing so much away.' Many of Gladstone's friends and the press thought he was seriously lacking in judgement at this stage in his career, though he did not see the acceptance of the Ionian Islands commission as in any way a commitment to the Conservative government.

On his return to England following the general election when the Conservatives failed again to obtain a majority, there was the famous meeting at Willis's Rooms (see page 43) when a group of Whigs, Radicals and Peelites agreed to vote together to bring down Derby's government. 1859 proved to be a watershed in Gladstone's career. There was a clear choice: either he could accept office under Palmerston or face more years in the political wilderness, perhaps never to return. He was nearly 50, he wanted office again – there was little agonising this time. Gladstone explained his decision thus:

I felt sure that in finance there was still much useful work to be done. I was desirous to cooperate in settling the question of the franchise ... My friends were enlisted or I knew would enlist ... And the overwhelming interest ... of the Italian question ... joined to my entire mistrust of the former government in relation to it, led me to decide without one moment's hesitation.

Once Gladstone had accepted office in Palmerston's Liberal government and become Chancellor of the Exchequer for the second time, his party allegiance was really decided. To attempt a reconciliation with the Conservatives after this would have been political suicide: another change of party would have been regarded as treachery.

Why did Gladstone become Liberal leader?

A national politician

Gladstone's political allegiance may have been established in 1859 but this does not mean his accession to the leadership of the Liberals was by any means assured. A number of factors combined in the next few years to make this inevitable. One of the most important of these was the popularity and status as a national politician which he gained through his further work as Chancellor of the Exchequer.

In his second spell as Chancellor, between 1859 and 1866, Gladstone undoubtedly became the most popular politician in the country after Palmerston. In great part his popularity stemmed from his policies to which were attributed the economic prosperity of the country and the increasing standard of living.

Gladstone set out to introduce the programme he had drawn up while out of office. His priorities were:

To maintain a steady surplus of income over expenditure ...
  to lower indirect taxes –
  to simplify our fiscal system by concentrating ... on a few well chosen articles of extended consumption –
  and to conciliate support to the Income Tax by marking its temporary character and by associating it with beneficial changes in the laws.

Gladstone saw the Commercial Treaty with France, signed in 1860, as part of this programme, although it was initially the idea of Richard Cobden and was intended to repair relations between the two countries as much as to improve trade. Britain abolished duties on French silks and manufactured goods and lowered duties on French wines and brandy. France, for its part, fixed duties of no more than 30% on British textiles, coal, iron, and steel, to be reduced after three years to 25%. The treaty was certainly a great success for Britain: the value of British exports to France more than doubled in the ten years between 1859 and 1869. People knew that French wine was cheaper because of Gladstone.

Gladstone regarded his 1860 budget as his greatest. There were three main provisions:

◢ The income tax, which he had intended to abolish in this year, was raised by 1*d* to 10*d* in the £. This tax was now bringing in some £12 million annually and Gladstone needed to retain it in order to complete his abolition of protectionist tariffs, although he had written to his brother Robertson only a few months before: 'But let me own to you fairly that I am not converted in my general view of the tax itself. I view it as a grand instrument for war, and for special occasions, and for fixed reforms. But I shall rejoice to see the day when it may be dispensed with as an ordinary instrument of finance.'

◢ Duties were removed from a further 400 articles. This left only 15 with duties that raised any significant revenue.

◢ The excise duty on paper was to be abolished.

Gladstone gave a whole host of reasons why this so-called 'tax on knowledge' should be abolished, ranging from the need to revive rural paper works to the difficulties of defining exactly what was paper and collecting the duty. The proposal delighted the Radicals who had long campaigned for abolition, but the House of Lords vetoed the measure. In the constitutional conflict which ensued, Gladstone was clearly seen to be on the side of the Radicals. His popularity with 'the masses' began to grow even more. Gladstone solved the matter the following year by combining all the financial measures (including his Paper Bill) into a single bill which the Lords felt obliged to pass.

The repeal of the paper duty encouraged the growth not only of London newspapers, but of the provincial press. In 1854 there were only five provincial dailies with a combined circulation of 10,000 copies; just ten years later there were many more and their circulation was 438,000 per day. These 'penny dailies' were often owned by Liberals and were to be especially important for Gladstone's career.

A measure of which Gladstone was especially proud was the founding of Post Office Savings Banks which provided for the savings, however small, of ordinary people, with complete security, cheapness and convenience. Of course this was not his only intention: large sums of money were now made available to the Treasury quite independently of the Bank of England or the City, but Gladstone's popularity was enhanced yet further.

Popularity in the country

By the time Palmerston died in 1865, Gladstone was almost certainly the most popular politician in the country. Although there was a distinct amount of luck and even more opportunism involved in this, there seems little doubt that in the early 1860s Gladstone deliberately set about cultivating popular opinion. Until then his great speeches had been made in parliament. Starting with his tours of Lancashire and Tyneside in 1862, Gladstone began not only to travel widely, but also to speak to mass audiences. He was greatly assisted in his campaign by the growth of two particular nineteenth-century phenomena: the railways and the national and provincial press. The railways allowed him to travel frequently all over England, Scotland and Wales and his speeches were reported verbatim in the next day's newspapers. Already a household name among the middle classes, Gladstone became 'the People's William'.

The audiences at these speeches were largely working men, yet Gladstone often prepared for them more thoroughly than for any parliamentary speeches except the budgets. In April 1862 he spent large parts of the previous three days preparing for his Free Trade Hall speech in Manchester and took the unusual trouble to read it aloud to his wife before delivering it to the Association of Lancashire and Cheshire Mechanics Institutes. He visited factories all over the country and as Chancellor of the Exchequer received deputations from trade unions. He was able to give to working people the impression that he was on their side. This view was reinforced in May 1864 by his famous 'Pale of the Constitution' speech. Replying in the Commons to a bill to increase the borough franchise put forward by a radical MP Edward Baines, Gladstone praised 'the self-command, self-control, respect for order, patience under suffering, confidence in the law and regard for superiors' which, in his view, were characteristics of the working classes and therefore made them eligible to vote. He then went on make the statement which caused the sensation: 'I venture to say that every man who is not presumably incapacitated by some consideration of personal unfitness or of political danger, is morally entitled to come within the pale of the constitution.' Although Gladstone continued, 'Of course, in giving utterance to such a proposition I do not recede from the protest I have previously made against sudden, or violent, or excessive or intoxicating change' no one paid any attention to these qualifying words. It was widely believed that Gladstone was advocating universal suffrage. *The Times* accused him of using 'the language of sweeping and levelling democracy'. Gladstone had now firmly established himself as the friend of the working classes.

Manipulation of the press

Gladstone could rely on a favourable press because of his repeal of the paper duty. Newspapers, both national and provincial, became increasingly important to politicians during the second half of the nineteenth century as their readership grew, but Gladstone was the first politician to use the press deliberately and carefully to promote his popularity. He ensured regular press releases with details of his activities, and insisted his photograph be sold for 6*d* [2.5p] or less. Even when abroad, between 1858 and 1859, this continued, to the extent that Disraeli complained to the Colonial Secretary that: 'The daily advertisements respecting Gladstone, his intentions and movements, are becoming ridiculous. Please give direction that it be stopped.' Gladstone had particularly close links with *The Daily Telegraph* which had absorbed the old Peelite journal, *The Morning Chronicle*. Through his contacts with one of its reporters, Thornton Leigh Hunt, Gladstone began to 'leak' official information anonymously. He could always rely on the paper's support and indeed it was in *The Daily Telegraph* that the idea of 'the People's William' originated. From about 1862 onwards, the paper began to write of Gladstone as the future premier in editorials such as this:

> The time must come ... when the failing hand of the Premier will relinquish the helm of State. It would be ill for England, in prospect of such a day, if she had not one pilot at least to whom she could look with proud and happy confidence. She can, she does, so look to Mr GLADSTONE, because in all a long career of public life he has never swerved from the path of manly and straightforward policy.

The provincial press was equally fulsome in its praise. Staunchly Liberal newspaper owners like Joseph Cowen of *The Newcastle*

Chronicle, the leading daily paper in the north east, ensured a generous coverage of Gladstone's movements and speeches. The details of the Gladstones' 'royal progress', 'the Festival of Mr Gladstone', 'the Jubilee Day of the Tyne', when they steamed down the river accompanied by 12 boats carrying the local dignitaries and followed by a flotilla of smaller ships, the banks on either side packed with people, guns thundering and bells ringing – all this was noted by readers throughout the country.

The absence of rivals

It was undoubtedly a great asset to Gladstone in his quest for the Liberal leadership that there were no obvious rivals. In 1863 W. E. FORSTER noted that 'the want of the Liberal Party of a new man is great, and felt to be great; the old Whig leaders are worn out; there are no new Whigs; Cobden and Bright are impracticable and un-English, and there are hardly any hopeful Radicals. There is a great prize of power and influence to be aimed at.' It was fortuitous for Gladstone that, in the five years since 1859, some 12 ministers of cabinet rank had died. These included some who conceivably might have been contenders for the leadership. Aberdeen had died in 1860, Sidney Herbert, Gladstone's friend, regarded by some as a possible future leader, eight months later. Sir James Graham also died in 1861, leaving Gladstone and Cardwell as the only surviving Peelites. The ablest of the younger Whigs, George Cornewall Lewis, the Home Secretary, died in 1862 so that when Palmerston died in 1865 only Gladstone and LORD JOHN RUSSELL remained as possible leaders. Russell was already 73 and thinking of retirement. *The Times* published an editorial describing Gladstone as an alternative leader.

With Russell as Prime Minister in the Lords, Gladstone became leader of the House of Commons. His popularity outside the House of Commons was immense. During the Reform crisis, after the Liberal resignation, crowds roamed the London streets shouting, 'Gladstone for ever!' 'Gladstone and Liberty!' Even Nonconformists, hitherto alienated by Gladstone's High Church Anglicanism, were reconciled by his voting, in 1863, for the Burials Act which allowed Dissenters to hold funerals in parish graveyards and by his vote against church rates in 1866. Additionally, Gladstone began attending a series of meetings with Methodists and Congregationalists arranged by a Congregationalist minister he had come to know quite well. Thus it was that when, in December 1867, Russell announced his intention not to seek office again Gladstone inevitably became the next leader of the Liberal Party.

Profiles
WILLIAM EDWARD FORSTER (1819–86)

MP for Bradford (1861–86); Under-Secretary for the Colonies (1865–66); as Vice President of the Education Committee of the Privy Council, author of the Elementary Education Act, 1870; carried Ballot Act through Commons, 1872; Chief Secretary for Ireland (1880–82); broke with Gladstone over Irish policy and opposed Home Rule.

LORD JOHN RUSSELL, CREATED 1ST EARL RUSSELL 1861 (1792–1878)

Third son of the Duke of Bedford; educated by tutors and at Edinburgh University; Whig MP for Tavistock, 1813; champion of parliamentary reform and responsible for drafting the First Reform Bill, 1831; as Home Secretary (1835–39) responsible for Municipal Corporation Act and reducing number of crimes punishable by death; Prime Minister (1846–52); Foreign Secretary (1852–53) and cabinet minister in Aberdeen Coalition; Foreign Minister again under Palmerston (1859–65); Prime Minister again (1865–66).

Note taking

Note taking requires you to:

◢ *understand* the subject matter

◢ *select* the important ideas and information

◢ *organise* that material into a structured format which you will find easy to understand later on.

Make sure you are clear about the *purpose* of your notes.
Are they *short term* (e.g. for an essay) or *long term* (e.g. for revision later in the course)?
The *content* of these different types of notes might not be the same.

To make your notes clear and easy to follow, use:

◢ main headings

◢ side headings

◢ numbered points

◢ spacing

◢ indenting

◢ underlining.

Use abbreviations to save time and space, for example:

C19th	for the nineteenth century
c	about
ind	industrial
rev	revolution

You are bound to come up with your own personal ones.

Read this chapter again and **make brief notes** to explain how Gladstone moved from the Tory Party to the Liberal Party. Use the headings in the chapter as guides.

CHAPTER TWO

GLADSTONIAN LIBERALISM

Objectives
◢ To understand the ideas and make up of the Gladstonian
  Liberal Party
◢ To distinguish particular features of Gladstonian Liberalism.

According to tradition, the infant Liberal Party was born in the after-noon of 6 June 1859 in Willis's Rooms. It was here, at a meeting attended by 274 MPs, that Palmerston and Russell agreed to end their differences and declared their willingness each to serve under the other. At the same time Whigs, Radicals and Peelites agreed to vote together to bring down Derby's minority Conservative government. This they did four days later and Palmerston subsequently became Prime Minister of a Liberal government. It is important to note, how-ever, that those meeting at Willis's Rooms did not take their decisions with any intention of creating a new political party. It was merely a case of short-term tactics in parliament in order to regain office. Gladstone himself did not attend the meeting at Willis's Rooms and in fact voted *with* the Conservatives in the Commons on 10 June. His rea-sons for doing so are obscure and the other leading Peelites voted *against* the Conservatives. It has been suggested that Gladstone's vote arose out of a mistaken or self-indulgent loyalty to the past, or perhaps he wanted to maintain a degree of independence and was not yet ready to join any major grouping on a permanent basis.

However, as we have seen, Gladstone was quick to accept the post of Chancellor of the Exchequer under Palmerston and after this did not seriously entertain the idea of a return to the Conservatives. Although he disliked Palmerston, his dislike of Disraeli was greater. Gladstone explained his decision by saying he took office for the sake of the coun-try and because on foreign policy he was 'in real and close harmony with the new premier'. Others might describe it as ambition and the desire for office again. Nevertheless, in many respects Palmerston's administration was more Whig than Liberal: it was not until the mid 1860s that the Liberal Party emerged as a *bona fide* political party in parliament, (though even then, not united and disciplined in the modern sense). The Liberals were more organised in the country with

Liberal associations springing up, particularly in the manufacturing areas of the midlands and the north (e.g. Manchester in 1862 and Birmingham in 1865).

There is no debate, however, about the party Gladstone led to victory in 1868. This was not only the Liberal Party, but became known as the Gladstonian Liberal Party so closely were its members and their ideas identified with their leader. But for a better understanding of both Gladstone and his party we need to look more closely at those people who may be described as Liberals in the mid nineteenth century.

Who were the Liberals?

The customary convenient division of the Gladstonian Liberal Party into Whigs, Radicals and Moderates greatly oversimplifies the many groups, from many diverse origins, with different ideas and ideals, and sometimes contradictory aims, which came together under Gladstone's leadership. Some individuals are difficult to categorise and indeed a number of key personalities would fit into several categories.

Whigs and aristocrats

Although relatively few in number, the Whigs were still important and influential, especially in the early years of Gladstonian Liberalism. They were a clique of wealthy, aristocratic landowners who formed the right wing of the party yet who had a tradition of supporting reform, having been responsible for the Great Reform Act of 1832. They were used to holding office and had come to believe that such was their right. Under Gladstone they continued to dominate Liberal cabinets until most left the party over Home Rule in 1886. Eight of the 14 members of Gladstone's first cabinet can be described as Whigs including the Earl of Clarendon, Foreign Secretary, the EARL OF GRANVILLE, Secretary for the Colonies, the Duke of Argyll, Secretary for India and the MARQUIS OF HARTINGTON, Postmaster General. There might have been more had not some former cabinet ministers, such as Russell, declined to serve. When Gladstone resigned the leadership of the Liberal Party in January 1875, it was led by two Whigs – Granville in the Lords and Hartington in the Commons.

Despite his mercantile background, it was with the Whigs that

Gladstone was the most friendly out of all the groups in the Liberal Party. He himself married into a Whig family, and his son Willy married a granddaughter of his friend, the Duchess of Sutherland. His niece, brought up in the Gladstone household since her mother's death, married Lord Frederick Cavendish, Hartington's younger brother. Gladstone and his wife spent weekends at the great country houses of the Whig aristocrats and when he went on his speaking tours, it was in these houses that he stayed. Yet Gladstone never felt that he was one of them, despite being a considerable landowner, and the Whig view was that he was still 'Liverpool underneath'.

Profiles
GRANVILLE GEORGE LEVESON-GOWER, 2ND EARL OF GRANVILLE (1815–91)

Educated Eton and Christ Church, Oxford; MP 1836 until 1846 when he succeeded to the peerage; Foreign Secretary (1851–52; 1870–74; 1880–85); leader of the Liberal Party in the House of Lords from 1855; stayed loyal to Gladstone over Home Rule.

SPENCER CAVENDISH, MARQUIS OF HARTINGTON (1833–1908)

Succeeded to title as heir to the Duke of Devonshire, 1858; became MP in 1857; Postmaster General and Chief Secretary for Ireland in Gladstone's first cabinet; leader of the Liberals jointly with Granville (1875–80); Secretary for India (1880–82) and Secretary for War (1882–85); opposed Home Rule in 1886 and became leader of Unionists; became 8th Duke of Devonshire 1891 and went to Lords; served in Conservative and Unionist government (1895–1903).

The Whigs' importance lay in parliament rather than the country. They were a large and important group in the Lords where they were crucial as virtually the only supporters the Liberals had there. In the Commons they were less important and fewer in number. John Vincent in *The Formation of the British Liberal Party* (Constable, 1966) identifies only 27 Whig backbenchers in the House of Commons between 1859 and 1874; but other historians think his definition of Whig is an unduly narrow one and estimate more than this.

Radicals

The Radicals also were a relatively small group in the House of Commons. Some estimates put their number as low as a figure in the fifties. Once again there is a difficulty in defining exactly *who* was a Radical. Radicals did not necessarily vote together on an issue. Many were members of pressure groups concerned with such matters as the extension of the franchise, *dis-establishment* of the Church of England or the promotion of trade unions. Some represented pressure groups concerned with single issues – for example, land reform, temperance reform or compulsory State education – and were interested in their own narrow issue to the exclusion of all others. They were known as 'Faddists' in Victorian times – a term of disparagement. Yet other Radicals involved themselves in almost every cause.

There was a fundamental difference among Radicals over foreign affairs. Some, led by John Bright, were pacifists. They believed that Britain's involvement with other countries would inevitably lead to war which was morally wrong, bad for trade and hence the wealth of the country. Others believed that it was Britain's duty to intervene, militarily if necessary, to help liberals and nationalists abroad. Despite their differences and sometimes uncompromising stances, the Radicals were united to the extent that they were the one section of the Liberal Party genuinely and fervently committed to challenging the established order in Church and State. Gladstone needed the support of the Radicals in the House of Commons and he appointed John Bright to his first cabinet as President of the Board of Trade. The Radicals, for their part, looked to Gladstone, even more so following his measures as Chancellor of the Exchequer and his speaking tours in the north, as the leader who would carry out the reforms they wanted.

Outside parliament, Radicals were far more numerous: important in local government, in local Liberal associations and in forming the many political pressure groups demanding changes in society. Their support was crucial for Liberal election victories.

KEY TERM

Dis-establishment means ending the Anglican Church's special position as the official State Church (e.g. its bishops would no longer have the right to sit in the House of Lords).

Nonconformists

Many Radicals were also Nonconformists, a group which supported the Liberal Party in large numbers. The 1851 religious census showed about half the church-going population were Nonconformists and Nonconformity encompassed a wide social spectrum from wealthy manufacturers to craftsmen, artisans and small shopkeepers. Compared with its popularity in the country, Nonconformity was greatly under-represented in the House of Commons: the great majority of Liberal MPs were Anglicans. In the 1868 election only 64 of the 382 Liberal MPs were Nonconformists and of them, only John Bright, a Quaker, was in the cabinet.

It was to be expected that the Nonconformists would support the Liberals as they recalled that their predecessors, the Whigs, had pleased Dissenters by repealing the Test and Corporation Acts, commuting the Tithes and legalising Nonconformist marriages in the 1830s. They identified with Gladstone because of his Liverpool background, evangelical upbringing and his conspicuous morality. Gladstone's insistence that Christian principles should direct political decisions and his enthusiasm for leading national crusades on great moral issues particularly attracted the Nonconformists. Gladstone, for his part, recognised the importance of the Nonconformists when he said, in 1877, 'Nonconformity supplies the backbone of English Liberalism.'

The concerns of the mid-nineteenth century Nonconformists can be seen by studying the pressure groups they established to promote their causes. They also illustrate that quality which came to be called the 'Nonconformist Conscience'.

The Liberation Society

This was the Society for the Liberation of Religion from State Patronage and Control. Formed in 1853, it grew out of the earlier Anti-State Church Association and was led by Edward Miall, a Congregationalist minister who was MP for Bradford (1869–74). It campaigned for the dis-establishment of the Anglican Church and was well organised with paid agents and speakers to canvass support; it sought to influence Liberal candidates in elections and it worked to ensure that all its supporters eligible to vote were registered. Miall was the editor of their official newspaper, *The Liberator*.

The National Education League

This pressure group was founded in Birmingham in 1869 by Joseph Chamberlain to campaign for a State education system that was undenominational, compulsory and free. He claimed that dis-establishment would release £90 million from endowments which would pay for it. The League soon became a flourishing pressure group with a hundred branches, an annual income of more than £6,000 and a newsletter with a circulation of more than 20,000. It was particularly strong in the north and the midlands as indeed was Nonconformity itself.

The United Kingdom Alliance

This pressure group was founded in 1853 to crusade for the restriction of the sale of alcoholic drink. It was dominated by Nonconformists, many of whom regarded drunkenness as the single greatest cause of human misery and poverty. It campaigned for the 'local option' which meant the right of ratepayers to veto the granting of licences for public houses in their area. This too was a vigorous pressure group with a staff of 30, an annual income of £13,000 and a weekly paper, *The Alliance News*, with a circulation of 25,000. In 1865 there were only two total abstainers in the Commons, Edward Baines and Benjamin Whitworth, but by 1885 there were as many as 36.

The Nonconformists were important because they pushed issues like dis-establishment and temperance to the top of the Liberal agenda, and while Gladstone made dis-establishment in Ireland the focal point of his 1868 election campaign, he had no particular sympathy for the temperance movement and himself enjoyed drinking fine wines and champagne. The influence of the Nonconformists in the Liberal Party can be seen later in the century when their pressure helped to keep Sir Charles Dilke out of the cabinet in 1886 following his involvement in a divorce case. Their influence was perhaps even more significant when, following another divorce case, Charles Stewart Parnell, the leader of the Irish Party, was found guilty of adultery. The *Methodist Times* declared that no Methodist would vote for the Liberals if they allowed an adulterer to remain leader of a political party (see Chapter 6).

Middle-class manufacturers

Victorian Liberalism was essentially an urban movement: the Party was well supported in the industrial areas of the midlands and the north and we have seen that the two largest of the growing towns, Manchester and Birmingham, played leading roles in the development of Liberalism. It is perhaps surprising, in view of this, that there were relatively few middle-class manufacturers in the House of Commons. In his work, *The Liberal Ascendancy, 1830–1886*, T. A. Jenkins estimates that in 1869 there were 86 Liberal MPs who could be classified as merchants and manufacturers. By 1874, there were 72 and by 1886, there were 102. This relatively slow growth and these low numbers can be accounted for in two ways: until the Redistribution Act of 1885 the industrial towns were still badly under-represented in terms of seats. Secondly, many factory and mill owners did not feel they could spare weeks on end in London to attend the House of Commons. They were more likely to fulfil political ambitions by going into local politics where there was usually ample opportunity to gain power and status without leaving their businesses.

Nevertheless, some leading industrialists did enter parliament on behalf of the Liberal Party – some of whose names are still recognisable today:

Michael Bass	Burton-on-Trent brewer, MP for Derby (1848–83)
Jeremiah Colman	Norwich mustard maker, MP for Norwich (1871–95)
Sir Francis Crossley	Halifax carpet maker, MP for Halifax (1852–59) and West Riding of Yorkshire (1859–72)
George Palmer	Reading biscuit maker, MP for Reading (1878–85)

There were others whose goods were household names in Victorian times, such as:

Samuel Morley	Nottingham hosiery maker, MP for Bristol (1868–85)
A. J. Mundella	Nottingham hosiery maker, MP for Sheffield (1868–97)

Sir Titus Salt   Yorkshire worsted maker, MP for Bradford
                    (1859–61)

As well as being highly successful industrialists, these men were able to make their own distinctive contribution to both Liberalism and the Liberal Party.

Skilled workers

Artisans were loyal and enthusiastic supporters of both the Liberal Party and Gladstone. These skilled workers voted Liberal in large numbers. Poll books (the official records of how each elector cast his votes) were kept in each constituency prior to the Ballot Act of 1872. From these we can tell that in almost every constituency, whether rural or urban, large or small, artisans were the group which most loyally supported the Liberal Party. We find that the working-class Liberal electors tended to be craftsmen, like shoemakers and cobblers, tailors, furniture makers and building craftsmen. Such men had often been active in reform pressure groups and the Chartist movement and were keenly interested in politics. More recently they enjoyed a rise in their standard of living which they attributed directly to Gladstone's policies as Chancellor of the Exchequer. Such men were obviously going to support Liberal policies like low taxation and reduction of tariffs.

The motives for supporting the Liberals were not just economic however; great numbers of the working class believed that Gladstone had a unique understanding of their needs and aspirations. His many speeches encouraged them in this belief, as did his appreciative comments on his many visits to factories and his reception of trade union delegations. Gladstone certainly cultivated working-class support, but how far he had their particular interests at heart is debatable. Speaking in the reform debate in 1866, Gladstone said: 'I believe the composition of the House might be greatly improved; and that the increased representation of the working classes would supply us more largely with the description of members we want, who could look not to the interests of classes, but to the public interest.' On the other hand, he was aware that fluctuations of trade often had an adverse effect on the standard of living of many working-class people. He suggested to Robert Lowe, the Chancellor of the Exchequer, that he should draw up a cost of living index in order to compare the living standards of the

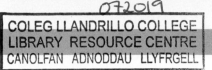
working classes in 1832, 1852 and 1872. The list of items he drew up for costing, however, tells us more about Gladstone's priorities than those of the working class – lodging, fuel, clothing, food, travel, books and newspapers.

The first working-class MPs to be elected were the Liberals Thomas Burt and Alexander MacDonald in 1874, but the working classes had their own agenda in terms of trade union rights, and hours and conditions of work. As the end of the century approached, many of them began to believe that these interests would be better served by their own political party rather than the Liberal Party.

Writers and intellectuals

Though relatively few in number, this group was disproportionately influential. The role of writers and intellectuals in conceiving and disseminating Liberal ideas and instigating debate was of vital importance.

The best known of this group was undoubtedly John Stuart Mill, the philosopher, whose most famous work, *On Liberty*, was published in 1859. Also influential in their time were *Considerations on Representative Government* (1861), *Essays on Reform* (1867) and *The Subjection of Women* (1869) in which he argued for women's suffrage. As early as 1839 Mill had argued for the creation of a new Liberal Party to be supported by what he called the non-aristocratic professions (e.g. teaching, medicine, engineering, and journalism) to advocate middle-class rather than universal suffrage. Mill believed the working classes were not yet sufficiently educated to receive the vote, though they would be one day. This idea became central to the Liberal creed. The vote was not so much a right as a trust to be earned. Meanwhile the educated middle classes should govern on behalf of the working classes.

John Stuart Mill entered parliament as MP for Westminster in 1865. Other writers who became Liberal MPs were John Acton, the Cambridge historian (Carlow, 1859–65) and Thomas Hughes, the author of *Tom Brown's Schooldays* (Lambeth, 1865–68). Anthony Trollope contested Beverley in 1868 but was unsuccessful. Two other novelists active in support of the Liberals at this time were Charles Dickens and William Makepeace Thackeray. Both were active in a

Liberal pressure group, the Administrative Reform Association (see page 53). Thackeray actually contested Oxford for the Liberals in 1857 but was not elected. Trollope, together with two other novelists, George Eliot and George Meredith, set up in 1865 *The Fortnightly Review*, a Liberal periodical which became the leading political review in the country with a circulation of 25,000 by 1872.

Writers and intellectuals wanted a tolerant and open society; they wanted reform of higher education which they considered narrow and exclusive; they also wanted to replace property with intellect as the qualification for government. These became important Liberal ideas.

What were the distinctive features of Gladstonian Liberalism?

The members of the Victorian Liberal Party in parliament and its supporters in the country were people of very varied backgrounds, but they were brought and held together by more than mere political expediency or Gladstone's charismatic leadership. There were common ideas and values which went beyond the narrow aims and sectional interests of some individuals and pressure groups. Together these made up the Liberal ideology.

Liberty

The word 'liberal' has its derivation in the Latin adjective *liber*, which means free, unrestricted, or open. An intense commitment to the ideal of liberty lay at the heart of Gladstonian Liberalism. This love of freedom permeated all areas of Liberal philosophy, for example:

◢ freedom for individuals and businesses to manage their affairs without the interference of the State
◢ freedom of worship and of speech
◢ freedom of the press
◢ economic freedom – to trade without protective restrictions
◢ freedom for national groups to rule themselves.

Good government and administrative competence

The Liberals believed that the State should involve itself as little as possible in the lives of its citizens: they and Gladstone saw a much more limited role for the State than we have today where it interferes in almost every area of our lives. They did not see it as the role of government to manage the economy or provide social welfare, much less decree what should be taught in schools! They did consider that those functions the State did undertake should be carried out as efficiently as possible. Indeed it could be said that this belief helped to bring about the Liberal Party because Gladstone and the Peelites became so exasperated with the Conservatives' financial incompetence. Many middle-class Liberals believed the administration of the country would be more effective if the civil service were to be administered by officers appointed on merit, rather than aristocratic background and family connections. Samuel Morley set up the Administrative Reform Association to campaign for this. Promotion by talent rather than by patronage became one of the enduring principles of Victorian Liberalism. Nonconformists were particularly keen to see honesty and integrity in public life and this fitted with Gladstone's view of government as a moral trust from God.

Public economy and low taxation

Next to efficiency, Victorian Liberals valued economy. Good government was synonymous with cheap government. Nonconformists thought large spending extravagant and immoral; businessmen and industrialists wanted low rates and taxes. Jokes about candle ends and cheeseparing notwithstanding, Gladstone waged a continual war against waste in government. In his view, undue public expenditure was 'not only a pecuniary waste, but a great political, and above all, a great moral evil'. Those limited services which only the State could supply must be provided at the lowest possible cost. Gladstone called it retrenchment. He even ordered that the addresses on the labels on diplomatic bags be scratched out so that they could be reused. Along with public economy went low taxation and we saw in the last chapter how Gladstone applied Liberal principles in his budgets.

Free trade and peace abroad

Free trade was an article of faith for Victorian Liberals. Gladstone, as Peel's foremost disciple, was devoted to free trade. It was a rallying cry which united all the groups in the Liberal Party. After 1846, individuals might still have considered themselves to be primarily Radicals, Whigs or Peelites, but they were linked by a common bond, the cause of free trade. Radicals had long been attached to the cause: it had been part of the **Benthamite** agenda; many Nonconformists argued that freedom of trade was a moral issue, just like freedom of religion. Anti-Corn Law League orators like Cobden and Bright regularly spoke in biblical metaphors. It was true, of course, that many Nonconformists were also industrialists and there was a degree of self interest in seeing an increased volume of trade, higher profits and at the same time lower prices for their workers. For Gladstone free trade was undoubtedly a moral issue and he maintained his support for it until the end of his career. In 1890 he wrote 'all protection is morally as well as economically bad'.

KEY TERM

Benthamite was the term used to describe followers of Jeremy Bentham (1748–1832), philosopher, friend of James Mill. Bentham put forward the idea that all government and institutions should be tested in the light of *the greatest happiness of the greatest number*. He was also the author of utilitarianism.

For the Liberals, free trade had another importance, for they believed that not only would it lead to greater prosperity for everyone in Britain, but the consequent growth in international trade would automatically mean closer cooperation between nations and an end to war. Gladstone seems to have agreed with this view for, at the time of the Commercial Treaty with France, he told Cobden: 'Neither you nor I attach for the moment any superlative value to this Treaty for the sake of the extension of British trade ... What I look to is the social good, the benefit to the relations of the two countries, and the effect on the peace of Europe.' To Radicals and Nonconformists war was abhorrent and evil: disputes should be settled by arbitration. They may accurately be described as pacifists. The Peace Society, formed by the Quakers in 1816, became an important Liberal pressure group in the 1850s and 1860s.

For Gladstone, of course, there was another reason for pursuing a peaceful foreign policy – an active foreign policy was expensive. Defence spending was the largest item of government expenditure in the 1850s and 1860s apart from the interest on the national debt. Together these two accounted for more than three-quarters of all government spending. Gladstone also thought that keeping large standing armies was dangerous and could actually lead to war. This was one of the reasons why the Liberals were anti-imperialists, partly in line with the view current at the time that colonies were a drain on resources, but also because of the immorality of ruling other peoples. John Bright described British rule in India as 'ambition, conquest and crime'. Despite the strong identification of the Liberal Party with peace and non-intervention, there was also a simultaneous, and incompatible, desire on the part of many Liberals to support nationalist groups abroad struggling for their freedom. John Stuart Mill argued this case particularly strongly and said that a Liberal government should 'assist struggling liberalism, by mediation, by money or by arms, wherever it can prudently do so'. Gladstone too, had much sympathy for 'the cause of nations rightly struggling to be free' and he had the unenviable task of marrying two contradictory principles. His solution was that 'interference in foreign countries should be rare, deliberate, decisive in character, and effectual for its end'. He was to find the burden of putting principles into practice a difficult one (see Chapter 4).

Voluntaryism

Voluntaryism was a fundamental Victorian idea and it describes more precisely the Gladstonian Liberal philosophy than the term *laissez-faire* which is often used. To Liberals good government meant cheap and limited government. They recognised the evils of poverty, disease and illiteracy around them but believed that these could be effectively alleviated not by the State, but by the voluntary actions of individuals and groups, paid for by charitable donations. Gladstone wrote to Bright in 1873, 'for myself, not in education only, but in all things, I prefer voluntary to legal machinery, when the thing can be well done either way'.

Gladstone believed it was morally right for the State to intervene only when and where voluntary activity was demonstrably ineffective. We have already seen such an instance when, in 1861, he introduced the Post Office Savings Bill because he distrusted the existing banking system and wanted the poor to have greater security for their savings than friendly societies provided.

Ideally, Victorian Liberals believed that it was the responsibility of the individual to provide for his family. There was a widespread notion that poverty was the result of fecklessness and that destitution came about through improvidence. This view was much encouraged by a nineteenth-century bestseller, Samuel Smiles' *Self Help*, published in 1859. It was a collection of biographies of successful men who had achieved their success, according to Smiles, by their own efforts. These uplifting tales were interspersed with short homilies as, for example:

No laws, however stringent, can make the idle industrious, the thriftless provident, or the drunken sober. Such reforms can only be effected by means of individual action, economy and self-denial, by better habits rather than by greater rights.

Thus if the State helped an individual it would weaken his moral fibre and it would be unfair to those who *had* saved or insured against illness or old age.

Gladstonian Liberal ideas are well illustrated by the Charity Organisation Society founded in 1869 to administer charitable relief in London and supported by Gladstone himself. The society's aim was 'the promotion of habits of providence and self-reliance', and it distinguished between the deserving and undeserving poor. Only the deserving poor would be helped by charity, 'the idle, loafing, drinking class' would be directed to the workhouse. Yet the very existence of the Charity Organisation Society indicates a realisation that there was a need for some kind of central supervision and coordination of the various individual charities. As the century advanced, so an increasing number of Liberals began to question the idea that all poverty was necessarily the fault of individuals themselves. Although Gladstone himself remained committed to the voluntary principle and throughout his life gave a minimum of 10% of his wealth annually in charitable donations (sometimes as much as 14%), he accepted, albeit reluctantly, that there were times when State action was necessary. Nevertheless, this was the inferior option. At the end of his life, in 1890, he was commending the ideas of Andrew Carnegie from the *Gospel of Wealth* that the wealthy should give their surplus for the common good.

Optimism and improvement

A robust spirit of optimism inspired every area of Victorian Liberal thinking. Liberals confidently expected that the wealth generated by free trade would spread to every section of society and that private charity, friendly societies, cooperative movements and the like would eliminate any remaining poverty. There was a basic belief in the inherent goodness of human nature; a belief that everything was susceptible to improvement and that progress in all areas was certain. Liberal ideas and ideals only begin to be understandable in the light of this optimism. John Bright summed up this feeling in 1865 when he wrote: 'I believe the powers of good are gaining steadily on the powers of evil. I think it is eminently so in this country.'

Gladstone shared this optimism. As late as 1887 he wrote:

And the sum of the matter seems to be that upon the whole, and in a degree, we who lived 50, 60, 70 years back, and are living now, have lived into a gentler time; that the public conscience has grown more tender, as indeed was very needful ... that upon the whole the race has been reaping, and not scattering; earning and not wasting.

It is remarkable that Gladstone could sustain his optimism so late in his career and at a time when many Liberals were becoming increasingly pessimistic and when many believed their principles were being compromised. But this was in the future. In 1868, when Gladstone began to set about choosing the members of his first cabinet, Liberal optimism was at its height.

Reading for A-Level

If you are to achieve any grade beyond an E at A-Level, you will need to know more than can be learned from class notes and the textbook. These are good starting points, but wide and careful reading is absolutely *essential*. There are a number of different kinds of book which you will find useful.

◢ *Textbooks*   You will probably have been issued with a textbook at school or college, but this may not necessarily be the best one for every topic you have to study. If you are finding a particular topic difficult, it could well be useful to read a GCSE textbook which will deal with the topic in a clear and straightforward way. Other textbooks are aimed particularly at the needs of A-Level students. Some textbooks are aimed at university students, and are likely to offer you more detail than the others and probably assume a certain degree of knowledge at the outset. There are suggestions in each of these categories at the end of this book.

◢ *Topic books*   Publishers are now producing short and attractive topic books designed specifically for A-Level students. Some of these contain discussion of issues as well as narrative, plus documents, examination questions and helpful advice. As well as this series, look out for Access to History, Lancaster Pamphlets, Seminar Studies and British History in Perspective.

◢ *Monographs*   These are more specialised interpretations of important topics based on extensive research and often presenting a new and original view. You might refer to a work such as this when you have already covered the topic, to supplement your general reading or when researching for an essay. It is highly unlikely that you would need, or indeed want, to read such a book from cover to cover, but use of the table of contents and the index should help you find those parts most useful for your purpose. The last chapter can often be most rewarding in terms of ideas.

◢ *Biographies*   These can offer fascinating insights and really help you get to know and begin to understand the people you are dealing with. Do not be put off by the length of some of these. They can be very readable. There is no need to read every word! Use the index to find the most useful and relevant parts.

TASK

◢ *Study guides*   There are a number of revision guides which can be useful in the run up to exams. They are best used towards the end of your course when advice on how to revise and exam technique is particularly helpful.

◢ *Fiction*   There are a great many Victorian novels still in print and widely read today. These can provide you with some lighter reading and give you a real insight into social conditions and attitudes at the time. Gladstone's great rival, Disraeli, wrote novels which were bestsellers in their day. Charles Dickens, Anthony Trollope and George Eliot were Liberal sympathisers as well as bestselling novelists. If you are also a student of A-Level English, reading some of their works is likely to be doubly advantageous!

Look back over this chapter and check which individuals you feel you have only a sketchy acquaintance with. Use the recommended reading list on page 126 to help you find out more. Use the advice at the end of the last chapter to help you add to your notes.

CHAPTER THREE

GLADSTONIAN LIBERALISM IN PRACTICE

Objectives
◢ To consider the extent to which the reforms of Gladstone's first ministry were based on Liberal principles
◢ To explain why Gladstone and the Liberals lost the 1874 general election.

Gladstone's first cabinet

'One of the best instruments for government that ever was constructed'?

It was always likely that any ministry of Gladstone's would be an eventful one. Firstly, he had been a reforming Chancellor of the Exchequer; secondly, he felt a sense of urgency because, at 59, he did not expect to lead another. He often mentioned his forthcoming retirement in his diary. His views were summed up in a letter to Granville written fairly soon after the fall of his first ministry: 'My opinion is and has long been that the vital principle of the Liberal Party ... is action, and that nothing but action will ever make it worthy of the name of a party.' Before any action could take place, however, Gladstone had first to form his cabinet.

In constructing his first cabinet Gladstone chose colleagues to reflect all shades of Liberal opinion, but the balance reflected that of the parliamentary party, rather than the party in the country. Whigs held a disproportionate number of posts. Out of a total of 15, at least seven could be counted as Whigs, among them the EARL OF CLARENDON, Granville and Hartington. Besides Gladstone himself, there was another Peelite, EDWARD CARDWELL, and there was one Radical, John Bright. The inclusion of a man who was at one and the same time a Radical, a Nonconformist and a manufacturer marked a new departure in nineteenth-century cabinet making. Such a man would not previously have been considered fit for office. It was remarkable that he was prepared to sit in the same Cabinet as ROBERT LOWE, who became Chancellor of the Exchequer, for Lowe had aroused Bright's wrath when he spoke so forcibly against the Liberal Reform Bill in 1866.

Profiles

GEORGE VILLIERS, 4TH EARL OF CLARENDON (1800–70)

Born in London and held diplomatic posts in St Petersburg, France and Madrid; succeeded to the peerage, 1838; President of the Board of Trade, 1846; Lord-Lieutenant of Ireland (1847–52); Foreign Secretary (1853–58; 1865–66 and 1868–70).

EDWARD CARDWELL (1813–86)

Born into a wealthy merchant family in Liverpool; educated at Winchester and Balliol College, Oxford; entered parliament as a Peelite MP, 1842; President of the Board of Trade (1852–55); Chief Secretary for Ireland (1859–61); Chancellor of the Duchy of Lancaster (1861–64); Colonial Secretary (1864–66); Secretary for War (1868–74); created Viscount Cardwell, 1874, when he retired exhausted from working on the Army reforms.

ROBERT LOWE (1811–92)

Born near Nottingham, son of a clergyman; educated at Winchester and University College, Oxford; became a barrister and went to Australia in 1842 where he was a member of the New South Wales legislative council (1843–50); MP for Kidderminster (1852–59), Calne (1859–68) and London University (1868–80); Chancellor of the Exchequer (1868–73); Home Secretary (1873–74); opposed parliamentary reform; created Viscount Sherbrooke, 1880.

Although there were many shades of opinion among the members of Gladstone's first cabinet, what many of them had in common was the fact that they could be described as 'new men': neither Lowe nor Bright came from the landed aristocracy; nor could Goschen, Childers, Bruce, Cardwell or W. E. Forster (who joined the cabinet in 1870) be described as coming from the traditional political class. There is no doubt, however, that it was an outstandingly able cabinet – a fact which Gladstone himself recognised when he called it 'one of the best instruments for government that ever was constructed'.

Gladstone did not embark on his first ministry with a coherent reform programme already prepared. This is surprising in the light of the comprehensive programme he drew up before his return to office as Chancellor of the Exchequer. He did have his own legislative plans for Ireland (see Chapter 5) but apart from those he was prepared to leave his ministers to draw up proposals. Once these had been introduced and the government committed to them, he was prepared to add his own weight in the House to ensure their success. Gladstone's first ministry has been widely regarded as one of this country's greatest reforming ministries. The extent to which the legislation reflects the principles of Gladstonian Liberalism is perhaps more debatable.

Administrative reform

We have already seen how the desire for good government, efficiency and economy lay at the heart of Gladstonian Liberalism and these principles can be seen behind many of the reforms of Gladstone's first government. The Prime Minister was particularly interested in promoting administrative competence and had already, in 1853, appointed the Northcote-Trevelyan Committee with a brief to report on recruitment to the civil service. At that time patronage was still the route to a career there and civil servants, appointed to posts as a reward for political support or because they had the right aristocratic connections, too frequently proved to be idle or lacking in ability. The Administrative Reform Association, a pressure group founded in 1855 under the chairmanship of Samuel Morley to campaign for the talented middle class to enter the civil service, was an influential Liberal pressure group. Its view that 'the whole system of government is such as in any private business would lead to inevitable ruin' almost certainly accorded with Gladstone's own.

Gladstone was keen to implement the Northcote-Trevelyan report of 1855 which recommended a competitive examination to select civil servants. This fitted well with the Liberal Nonconformist and Radical notions of opposition to privilege, patronage and nepotism, but it is important to note that in no sense was this intended to be a democratic measure. There was no intention to open all posts to everyone. The civil service was divided into grades which roughly corresponded to the classes in society. The examination to recruit clerks for the lower grade encompassed such subjects as book-keeping, indexing, copying, English history, geography and the three 'R's. Examinations for the upper (administrative) grade were based on the kind of classical education acquired by a student at a public school and university. Thus the lower orders were effectively excluded. Nevertheless, many members of the aristocracy were opposed to the measure and Gladstone was obliged to exclude the Foreign Office from the reforms because of the opposition of his Foreign Secretary, Clarendon and Clarendon's successor, Granville.

Army reform

Next to efficiency, Gladstonian Liberals valued economy and the Army reforms of Gladstone's first ministry achieved both of these: both the size and efficiency of the army was increased at a reduced cost. Although the disasters of the Crimean War had vividly demonstrated the inadequacies of the British Army, any earlier attempts to reform had been blocked by Palmerston. Edward Cardwell, Gladstone's Peelite War Minister, already had proposals for change having sat on commissions of enquiry. Immediately on coming to office, he had abolished the practice of flogging in the Army during peace-time. This was essential if a career in the ranks was to be anything more than penal servitude for the dregs of the population. In the following year, 1869, Cardwell began withdrawing troops from the self-governing colonies which both saved money and provided more men at home (20,000 soldiers returned to the home establishment during 1870–71). The Franco-Prussian War which broke out in 1870 and the subsequent victories of the Prussian military machine at Metz and Sedan further stressed the urgent need for reform.

Cardwell, supported by Gladstone, brought forward his Army Regulation Bill in 1871 which proposed to abolish the system whereby commissions were purchased – a system which allowed young men from rich families to buy positions as officers in the army. The cost of buying a captaincy in the Life Guards for instance was £3,500. This resulted in promotion according to wealth, rather than merit, and many officers held ranks for which they were untrained and unfitted. Such purchase had already been made illegal in 1809 except where it was regulated and the price kept under control by royal warrant (which had since spread to cover practically all commissions). Many landed gentry arrived at their positions in either the Lords or the Commons via a command in the Army so there was understandably considerable opposition to Cardwell's bill in both Houses, but especially in the

Lords where it was rejected. The Commander-in-Chief, the Queen's cousin, the Duke of Cambridge, was opposed to all change. Such opposition confirmed Gladstone in his opinion that the upper classes were selfish and lacking in moral sense, a theme to which he was to return on a number of occasions. In a speech to his Greenwich constituents in October he said that 'in attacking purchase in the Army, we were perfectly aware that we were assailing class interest in its favourite and most formidable stronghold'.

Meanwhile, when he was in danger of losing the Bill, Gladstone decided to ask the Queen to withdraw the royal warrant which would have meant the end of the purchase of commissions, but without the compensation for officers provided for in Cardwell's Bill. Rather than lose the compensation, the Lords passed the Bill. Although Army officers continued to be drawn almost exclusively from the landed classes, within their number promotion in future came to depend on ability. For Cardwell this marked only the beginning: during the remainder of the ministry he embarked on a whole series of reforms which were to modernise the British Army. Among these were:

- the introduction of short service: six years with the colours and six in the reserves;
- the re-arming of the infantry with the first satisfactory breech loading rifle, the Martini-Henry;
- the reorganisation of regiments (previously known only by numbers) on a territorial basis, each county having its own regiment of two linked battalions, one on active service overseas, the other in training at home;
- the subordination of Commander-in-Chief to the Secretary of State for War, thus recognising the supremacy of parliament over the Army;
- the reorganisation of the War Office into three departments, each responsible to the Secretary of State;
- the development of military education at Woolwich, Sandhurst and the Staff College, Camberley.

As a result of Cardwell's measures the Army increased by 25 battalions and 156 horse-drawn field guns, an Army career became more attractive and the reserves increased from just 3,500 to almost 36,000.

Britain had the beginnings of a modern professional army and this was all achieved at no extra expense: Cardwell left the estimates lower than he found them – a triumph of Liberal efficiency and economy!

Law reform

The Gladstonian Liberal passion for order and efficiency is also illustrated in the legal reforms which were the work of the EARL OF SELBORNE, whom Gladstone appointed Lord Chancellor in 1872. The English legal system had developed haphazardly over the years, many of the structures and institutions dating from the Middle Ages. Actually two legal systems had grown up side by side: common law, which was based on ancient rights and customs and decisions made by judges on previous occasions, not written down and dispensed in one set of courts; and equity, a more rigid body of rules, dispensed in another. New courts had been created in a random way to meet different needs; as a consequence the administration of justice was slow and in-efficient. Selborne's Judicature Act of 1873 streamlined things by providing that both equity and common law should be administered in every court by every judge and where their rules conflicted, those of equity should take precedence.

The Judicature Act of 1873 abolished:

◢ the three common law courts (Queen's Bench, Common Pleas and Exchequer) which dated from the time of Edward I
◢ the Courts of Chancery and Appeal in Chancery
◢ the High Court of Admiralty
◢ the Court of Probate and
◢ the Court of Divorce and Matrimonial Causes.

Profile ROUNDELL PALMER, 1ST EARL OF SELBORNE (1812–95)

Educated at Rugby and Winchester where he was friendly with Cardwell and Lowe, then Trinity College, Oxford; became an outstanding lawyer; MP for Richmond (1861–72); Solicitor General (1861–63); Attorney General (1863–66); created 1st Baron Selborne, 1872; and 1st Earl, 1881; Lord Chancellor (1872–74; 1880–85); responsible for the Married Women's Property Act, 1882; opposed and then broke with Gladstone over Home Rule.

All of the above were now united to form a single new court, the Supreme Court of Judicature, which was divided into the High Court and the Court of Appeal. Only the London Bankruptcy Court was left outside the system. This reform greatly simplified the administration of justice and was probably the least controversial of all the reforms of this ministry, although many peers objected to the abolition of the House of Lords' role as the final court of appeal. (Disraeli's government actually restored in 1876 the right of an individual to appeal to the House of Lords if dissatisfied with the verdict of a lower court.)

Education reform

The famous Elementary Education Act of 1870 illustrates another aspect of Gladstonian Liberalism: the willingness to approve government action where voluntary action clearly was not working. Ideally Gladstone would have preferred a wholly voluntary system of education, but by the latter half of the nineteenth century a number of factors had combined to impel State intervention. Of course the State was already involved to a certain extent. Since 1833 it had made an annual grant towards the provision of elementary education and by 1856 this sum had become so large – about £500,000 – that a Department of Education was created to deal with the administration involved. Education for the lower classes, however, was still provided almost exclusively by two voluntary bodies, the National Society for the Education of the Poor in the Principles of the Established Church (founded in 1811 and on whose council Gladstone had once sat), and the Nonconformist British and Foreign Schools Society. The vast majority of government grants went to National schools, but between 1841 and 1851 Nonconformists built 364 schools and founded a teacher training college with their own money. Nevertheless, many Liberals began to realise that a purely voluntary system could never provide adequate education for all children at a time when the population was growing so rapidly.

In 1858 a Royal Commission had been appointed under the chairmanship of the Duke of Newcastle to enquire 'into the present state of popular education in England, and to consider and report what measures, if any, are required for the extension of sound and cheap elementary instruction to all classes of the people'. The subsequent report revealed some shocking findings: about two-fifths of working-class children between six and ten were not attending school at all; of those who did, almost all left on or before their tenth birthday; many areas of the country had no schools and surveys in Manchester and Birmingham showed many parents could not afford school fees. The Commission received favourable reports on the education systems of other countries. Matthew Arnold, for instance, had been sent to investigate French, Swiss and Dutch provision. Some Liberals had long admired the State systems of others. Richard Cobden, for instance, as a result of two visits to the United States, was very impressed by the American system of universal secular education provided at public expense. Even the most committed voluntarists, led by Edward Baines, the influential proprietor of the *Leeds Mercury*, who once said 'it is not the duty or the province of the government to train the mind of the people', came to see the need for 'judiciously supplementing the present system of denominational education'. These last were the words of the National Education Union, a pressure group which came into existence in Manchester in 1869 and of which Baines was a member. This was the second group to be formed in that year. The first was the National Education League, one of whose leaders was the young Joseph Chamberlain. Its object was 'to rouse the whole country to a sense of our present educational destitution' and to fight for education 'universal, compulsory, unsectarian and free'.

A further impetus to government action was the Reform Act of 1867 which had given the vote to the urban working class. Robert Lowe voiced a widely held opinion when he said: 'I believe it will be absolutely necessary to compel our future masters to learn their letters.' Gladstone entrusted the task of preparing the education legislation to W. E. Forster, a former Quaker, who had long been interested in the subject. Introducing his Bill in the House of Commons, he said it had two aims: to cover the country with good schools and to get the parents to send their children to school. The apparently straightforward proposal to supplement the existing voluntary schools with board schools, paid for out of the rates, aroused a storm of protests from both Anglicans and Nonconformists. The resulting legislation was inevitably a compromise and satisfied neither faction.

> **Forster's Elementary Education Act of 1870**
>
> ◢ School Boards: local committees of 5–13 members elected by all ratepayers, including women, who would manage the new schools to be built where no others existed.
> ◢ School Boards to levy rates to meet part of the cost of Board Schools.
> ◢ Parents to pay fees and the rest of the cost to be met by government grants.
> ◢ Existing voluntary schools to receive increased government grants.
> ◢ Only simple Bible study in Board Schools, but parents who objected could withdraw their children.
> ◢ School Boards to pay the fees of poor children out of the rates whether they attended Board schools or voluntary schools.

Although the Act fell far short of the demands of the National Education League, in many ways it proved to be a success. It did bring elementary education within reach of all children. By the end of 1871, there were 300 School Boards and by 1876, over 1000. In the first six years 1,600 schools were built. State responsibility for education had been established, though the voluntarist principle had not yet been abandoned. It did arouse hostility from many Liberal supporters however, the repercussions of which were to be damaging for Gladstone and his government, as we shall see.

Gladstone himself was far more interested in higher education. He was, without a doubt, an elitist and could not really regard as educated a person who had not thoroughly studied ancient Greek and Latin. Many of his Nonconformist supporters saw the election victory in 1868 as their opportunity to press their own political agenda, one of whose priorities was the abolition of the university tests. Gladstone had been converted to the idea of admitting non-Anglicans to study and take first degrees at Oxford and Cambridge in the 1850s but they were still not eligible for scholarships, fellowships, teaching posts or membership of the governing bodies. Two private members' bills seeking to abolish the tests foundered early in the ministry but by then

Gladstone was convinced that they should go. He agreed to a government measure and himself introduced the bill in February 1871 using his considerable parliamentary skill to steer it through parliament, despite significant opposition in the Lords led by Salisbury. Although this legislation illustrates the influence of the Nonconformists in the Liberal Party, in fact its effects were limited because Dissenters preferred to set up their own colleges at Oxford. In any case Oxford and Cambridge no longer had a monopoly of higher education: colleges of London and Durham universities were now flourishing.

Other reforms
Licensing Act 1872

This was a reform long regarded as a classic example of Victorian Liberalism at work and yet it was a measure with which Gladstone himself had no sympathy. As a man who enjoyed both fine wine and strong beer, Gladstone believed it would have been hypocritical to seek to prevent others doing the same. His willingness to accept a measure he did not like tells us much about the importance of the Nonconformists within the Liberal Party. The uncontrolled sale of alcohol and the resulting drunkenness was undoubtedly a serious problem in Victorian towns and there was a strong temperance movement striving to persuade both individuals to abstain from alcohol and the government to legislate to restrict it. The United Kingdom Alliance (see Chapter 2) was particularly active in pressing for curbs on the drink trade and had its own spokesman in the Commons, Sir Wilfrid Lawson. Three MPs, Bright, Miall and Samuel Morley, were temperance lecturers and Edward Baines was the author of a bestselling pamphlet against drink. Lawson and another MP, William Caine, spent almost the whole of their parliamentary careers campaigning for temperance legislation. The pressure was so great that another MP, Sir George Trevelyan, on a speaking tour with Lawson said 'the Liberal Party must 'ere long become a temperance party'.

It was the job of the Home Secretary, Bruce, to prepare legislation to satisfy these demands. His first Bill, introduced in 1871, brought a storm of opposition from the liquor trade and did not satisfy the United Kingdom Alliance either, as it omitted their local veto. The following year a milder measure was passed introducing the following changes:

⊿ beer shops and ale houses in future must have a licence from the local magistrates;

⊿ some public houses would be closed down in areas where there were too many;

⊿ the closing hours of public houses were fixed at 11 o'clock in the country and midnight in London;

⊿ regulations were introduced to prevent the adulteration of drink (e.g. by putting salt in it).

Although the effects of the Licensing Act were undoubtedly beneficial, the Liberal Party became connected in the public mind with anti-drink legislation. This added to its ultimate unpopularity.

Trade union legislation 1871

At first sight the laws passed by Gladstone's first government affecting trade unions seem anything but liberal. One act recognised the legality of trade unions, but a second one, passed at the same time, made peaceful picketing illegal so that unions were virtually powerless to maintain a strike in order to bargain for improved pay and working conditions. The role of trade unions posed a dilemma for the Liberal government: Liberal principles were opposed to the 'monstrous tyranny exercised by the trades unions', but at the same time Gladstone had met a number of trade union deputations and been impressed by their 'responsibility'. Several Liberals did indeed support the infant trade union movement: A. J. Mundella, Samuel Morley and Thomas Hughes in particular worked for the recognition and protection of trade unions, with Hughes introducing a bill for this in 1869. This bill was withdrawn on the promise of a government one. Some Liberals, on the other hand, were opposed to unions, believing that they damaged the competitiveness of industry. Hostility had increased after the Sheffield outrages of 1866 which culminated in an explosion at the house of a non-union workman. The laws of the Home Secretary, Bruce, while giving protection to unions and their funds, were intended to protect individuals from this kind of intimidation. The result for the government, however, was the undiluted hostility of the trade union movement and a campaign for the repeal of the legislation led by the recently formed Trade Union Congress.

The Ballot Act 1872

Gladstone had no particular enthusiasm for voting in secret for he believed that a man should be independent and prepared to make his choice openly, but it was a cause dear to the hearts of the Radicals and he needed their support. Once convinced of the necessity for a bill, he gave it his wholehearted support and when it was thrown out by the Lords he denounced them for frustrating the will of the people's House. Threats of dissolution eventually assisted its passage. The effects of the law were to be far more profound in Ireland than on the mainland.

Why did Gladstone and the Liberals lose the 1874 election?

In March 1873 Gladstone's Irish Universities Bill (see Chapter 5) was defeated on its second reading. Many Liberals abstained and an unlikely combination of Conservatives plus 35 Irish Liberals and eight Radicals defeated the government by three votes. By this time Gladstone's government was both weary and disunited – Disraeli had already called the front bench 'a range of exhausted volcanoes'. Gladstone decided to resign, but Disraeli was unwilling to lead a minority government. Gladstone was obliged to resume office, but his government was fatally weakened. Lord Kimberley, the Colonial Secretary, wrote in his diary: 'Our old programme is completely exhausted: and Gladstone is not the man to govern without "measures", nor is he at all suited to lead a party in difficulties.' It is clear that Gladstone himself recognised the difficulties when he wrote: 'There is now no *cause*. No great public object on which the Liberal Party are agreed and combined.'

In an attempt to enhance the popularity of his government, Gladstone made a number of cabinet changes. Lowe, unpopular among both cabinet colleagues and backbenchers, was removed from the Chancellorship and sent to the Home Office. Bruce, whose handling of the Licensing Bill had been widely regarded as less than competent, was sent from the Home Office to the Lords. Bright, having recovered from his nervous breakdown, rejoined the cabinet to appease the Radicals. Gladstone himself took on the post of Chancellor of the Exchequer as well as the premiership. This gave him the opportunity to produce a budget which he hoped would both prove a rallying point for his party and a means to electoral success. He planned to abolish both the income tax and the sugar duties. Although the thriving economy was producing a substantial surplus, such a loss in government income required a saving somewhere to balance the budget. Gladstone decided to reduce defence spending by something between £600,000 and £1 million but there was strong opposition from some key cabinet members. Gladstone therefore decided, quite unexpectedly, on 24 January 1874, to go to the country. He hoped abolition of the income tax would be a vote winner and then, with an electoral mandate, the cabinet would reunite. This did not happen. The February general election brought a crushing defeat for the Liberals. To rub salt into the wound for Gladstone, although retaining his seat in Greenwich, he came only second to a young Tory gin-maker. As we shall see, some of the responsibility for this defeat lay with Gladstone despite – or perhaps because of – his reforming zeal.

Gladstone's leadership

First of all, Gladstone was not a party leader in the modern sense. The Liberal Party was a coalition of different groups and interests, but Gladstone did not really see it as his role to keep them together. In this respect he was a true disciple of Peel. Although he could go to considerable lengths to conciliate cabinet colleagues (he was particularly solicitous to Bright), he did not make any effort to keep in touch with his backbenchers. In his entire parliamentary life he dined only once in the House of Commons. Gladstone did not prepare his party, but called a snap election at a time when it was divided and demoralised. Since 1871 there had been a strong trend against the Liberals in by-elections and in the last eight months the Conservatives had won ten seats. Yet in these inauspicious circumstances, Gladstone chose not to use his greatest campaigning asset – his wonderful oratory. He made no great speeches to mass audiences of the kind he had made frequently in the 1860s. Neither did Gladstone make use of the press as he had done in the past. After 1868 he does not mention Thornton Hunt, the *Daily Telegraph* reporter with whom he had had close and frequent contacts, and although he had some contact with *The Times*, he seems to have fallen out with the London newspapers and indeed blamed them for some of the government's troubles. In a speech at Whitby in 1871 he said: 'A considerable section of the Metropolitan Press had discussed with greater severity the proceedings of parliament during the last Session than had been the case with the Provincial Press.' Although the *Telegraph* and *The Times* stayed loyal to Gladstone personally, there is no doubt that he missed an opportunity to promote Liberal policy and this may well have had an impact on the popularity of the government.

Unpopularity of the Liberal reforms
Although Gladstone wrote, 'We have been swept away, literally, by a torrent of gin and beer. Next to this comes education; that has denuded us on both sides for reasons dramatically opposite; with the Nonconformists, and the Irish voters', it is unlikely that the unpopularity of the new licensing laws were the main reason for Gladstone's defeat. Certainly, they antagonised the brewers and henceforth they supported the Conservative Party but, what is more important, his reforms tended to alienate the Liberal Party's natural supporters. The Nonconformists, for example, were still bitter about the Elementary Education Act which had confirmed government support for Anglican schools at their expense. Nonconformist abstentions were a severe blow to the Liberal Party. The working classes had little for which to thank the government: they too were angry about the restrictions on drinking and they were disappointed that Gladstone's government had done nothing for them in terms of living or working conditions. Trade unionists were so angry at the illegality of peaceful picketing that numbers of them abstained and some voted Conservative. The Labour Representation League ran 16 candidates of its own and captured two Liberal seats. Voters of all classes regarded Gladstone's foreign policy (see Chapter 4) as weak and failing to champion the national interest. This further increased the government's unpopularity.

The revival of the Conservative Party under Disraeli
An important reason for the Liberal defeat, and one which Gladstone underestimated, was the regeneration of the Conservative Party under Disraeli. First of all, Disraeli should be congratulated for his tactics at the time of Gladstone's first resignation in 1873. Ambitious though he was for power, he was not tempted to lead a minority government, but forced the Liberals to stay on until the Liberal government disintegrated further and his chance of electoral victory was more secure. The foun-

dations for success had been laid much earlier however, in 1870, when John Gorst was appointed Principal Party Agent. In this capacity he overhauled the party organisation, establishing a new headquarters which, by 1871, was called Central Office. There he installed the National Union to coordinate the work of constituency associations into which working men's clubs were incorporated, for he recognised the importance of the newly enfranchised urban voters.

Disraeli replaced Gladstone as the most influential public speaker of the day. Gorst organised mass meetings where Disraeli was able to display his charisma and oratorical powers to the full. The most important was at the Free Trade Hall in Manchester where he spoke for three-and-a-half hours to an audience of 6,000. Not only was it symbolically important, as it was held in a venue of special significance for his opponents, the Liberals, but his speech was important for its content too. He accused the Liberals of endangering national institutions, such as the Church of England, and he criticised Gladstone's foreign policy for its weakness in accepting Russia's repudiation of the Black Sea clause and paying damages to the United States over the *Alabama* (see page 84). According to Disraeli, he simply did not maintain Britain's prestige and he wanted to dispose of the colonies!

Disraeli's next great speech was at the Crystal Palace where he particularly identified his party with the working class and promised social reform. He said that *'no important step can be gained unless you can effect some reduction of their hours of labour and humanise their toil'* and that *'pure air, pure water, the inspection of unhealthy habitations, the adulteration of food, these and many kindred matters may legitimately be dealt with by the Legislature'*. Thus he made the Conservatives attractive to voters while constantly portraying the Liberals as dangerous: *'Not satisfied with the spoliation and anarchy of Ireland, they began to attack every institution and every interest, every class and every calling in the country.'* Not only were Disraeli's words appealing, he certainly sounded like a future (as well as a former) Prime Minister.

With Gladstone, however, must lie the balance of the responsibility for the defeat. The Liberals needed strong and firm leadership to hold them together. Gladstone had done this by the authority and force of his personality but by 1874 he was exhausted.

Role play

You will need about a fortnight to prepare for this – to do extra reading and research.

Half the group should take on the roles of Gladstone's ministers. If numbers are sufficient, each minister could have a civil servant. The rest of the group should be journalists questioning ministers about their reforms. Some suggestions for questioning are given below, but you need to think of supplementary questions and to be flexible, tailoring questions to the ministers' responses.

The Elementary Education Act 1870

Questions to William Forster, Minister for Education

Is it true that the Elementary Education Act has been brought forward because Britain has fallen behind its rivals such as Germany and the United States?

Surely it's enough to rely on voluntary schemes organised by the religious societies, as has been the case up to now?

How do you justify the additional expenditure, which will have to come from both local rates and central taxation?

Why have you banned denominational religious education in these new Board Schools?

Doesn't this new system leave the Church of England in a dominant position?

Why not scrap the Church schools altogether, and have a clear unified state system?

Should not something have been done for *secondary* education?

Civil service reform 1871

Questions to Robert Lowe, Chancellor of the Exchequer

Why do we need to change a tried and tested administrative system?

Do these changes to the civil service not represent an attack upon British traditions and the rights of property?

Is it true that the Foreign Secretary, the Earl of Granville, refused to allow this new system in the Foreign Office?

Why is it thought unsuitable for the Foreign Office?

Is competitive examination really the best method of recruitment?

How far will this principle now extend? Will MPs or government ministers have to undergo examinations?

The Ballot Act 1872

Questions to Lord Hatherley, the Lord Chancellor

For centuries Englishmen have cast their votes openly and in public. Surely there is something underhand and un-British about a secret ballot?

Isn't it perfectly appropriate for those who are better educated – landlords and employers – to influence and advise their inferiors on how to vote?

Have you considered the potentially dangerous implications of secret ballot in Ireland, where large numbers of poor tenants may be persuaded to vote for the recently formed Home Rule League?

This Act has clearly attracted much opposition – the first attempt was defeated in the House of Lords, and it is well known that a senior member of your party, the Marquis of Hartington, is strongly opposed. Why persist with an idea that may split your party?

We gather that candidates are still likely to try to bribe voters by means of free beer and transport – could the Act not have gone further and made bribery completely illegal?

The University Tests Act and the Public Health Act 1871–72

Questions to Lord Halifax, Lord Privy Seal

The Prime Minister is known to be a fervent Anglican and yet Lord Salisbury has claimed that the University Tests Act is a betrayal of the Church of England – do you agree with him?

Your government claims to believe in minimal State intervention, and yet the Public Health Act forces local authorities to employ a Medical Officer and staff – how do you justify this?

If public health is so important, why does the Public Health Act not clearly specify the compulsory duties of local health authorities?

CHAPTER FOUR

GLADSTONE'S FOREIGN POLICY

Objectives

◢ To distinguish the principles behind Gladstone's foreign policy and the stages by which he reached them

◢ To examine the extent to which Gladstone applied the principles in practice

◢ To consider to what extent Gladstone's foreign policy was successful.

Gladstone's 'right principles of foreign policy'

Few politicians have stated the principles that lay behind their policies as explicitly as did Gladstone when talking about his foreign policy. During a speech at West Calder, Scotland in 1879, when he was attacking Disraeli's foreign policy, Gladstone clearly defined 'what I think to be the right principles of foreign policy'. There were six principles:

1 *To foster the strength of the Empire by just legislation and economy at home ... and to reserve it for great and worthy occasions abroad.*

2 *To preserve to the nations of the world – and especially to the Christian nations of the world – the blessings of peace.*

3 *To strive to cultivate and maintain ... what is called the Concert of Europe; to keep the Powers of Europe in union together ... Because by keeping all in union together you neutralise and fetter and bind up the selfish aims of each.*

4 *Avoid needless and entangling engagements ... if you increase engagements without increasing strength you really reduce the Empire and do not increase it.*

5 *To acknowledge the equal rights of all nations.*

6 *The foreign policy of England should always be inspired by the love of freedom.*

A number of formative influences contributed to Gladstone's ideals.

Among these was his educational background: the study of the classics helped to shape his view of Europe. According to historian E. J. Feuchtwanger it gave him a 'deep sense of the continuity and universality of European civilisation'. Gladstone believed fervently in the Concert of Europe. To him this was not a mere form of words but a living reality. He really believed that, along with free trade, this was the best means of avoiding war. The idea was that representatives of the Great Powers should meet in congress or conference to reconcile the differing interests of members and that the combined influence of the others could tame the behaviour of a wayward power.

Gladstone had an enormous enthusiasm for Europe. Though he declined all invitations to visit the United States, he was an insatiable traveller and tourist on the continent of Europe, starting with the 'grand tour' undertaken with his brother in 1832 between leaving Oxford and entering the House of Commons. He did not regard the inhabitants of mainland Europe as foreigners to the extent that some of his compatriots did, perhaps because he was better able to communicate with them. Besides his fluency in Greek and Latin, Gladstone's French and Italian were both equal to the task of reading scholarly political works in the original languages and he spoke both well enough to make speeches to large and academic audiences.

Opposition to Palmerston's foreign policy

During most of Gladstone's pre-prime ministerial career, Palmerston was in charge of British foreign policy. Gladstone disliked and disapproved of Palmerston personally and he considered his policies to be as immoral as his lifestyle. Gunboat tactics and jingoistic speeches Gladstone found repellent and he first spoke out against both these aspects of Palmerstonian policy in 1840 when he criticised the latter's Opium War against China. This was Gladstone's first speech in the Commons on foreign policy. He called the war 'unjust' and he later confided to his diary: 'I am in dread of the judgements of God upon England for our national iniquity towards China.' Though it is true that in this particular instance he was probably influenced by the drug addiction of his sister Helen, we can already see Gladstone applying his principles of morality to foreign affairs.

Gladstone returned to his assault on Palmerston's foreign policy in

1850 when he made a three-hour speech in the Don Pacifico debate. David Pacifico was a Portuguese Jew and moneylender, whose house in Athens had been ransacked by a Greek mob in 1847. His claim for a massive £31,000 compensation had been rejected by the Greek government and, claiming British citizenship on the strength of his birth in Gibraltar, he sought the help of Britain. Palmerston, after threatening violence because Greece had failed to pay even the interest on the loans granted at the time of Greek independence in 1832, ordered a naval blockade on Piraeus, the port of Athens. He did this without consulting France or Russia, the other guarantors of Greek independence. It was not only Gladstone who regarded this reaction as excessive.

A censure motion was carried in the Upper House and there was a debate lasting four days and nights in the Commons. Defending himself, Palmerston declared that just:

as the Roman, in the days of old, held himself free from indignity when he could say Civis Romanus sum; so also a British subject, in whatever land he may be, shall feel confident that the watchful eye and the strong arm of England will protect him against injustice and wrong.

In reply Gladstone pointed out the difference between a Roman citizen and an Englishman. The former:

... was the member of a privileged caste; he belonged to a conquering race, to a nation that held all others bound down by the strong arm of power. For him there was to be an exceptional system of law; for him principles were to be asserted, and by him rights were to be enjoyed, that were denied to the rest of the world. Is that the view of the noble Lord as to the relation that is to subsist between England and other countries?

Thus Gladstone's ideas about morality in foreign affairs were established and made explicit at a relatively early stage in his career. On this occasion he was supported by the unlikely combination of Peel, Disraeli, Russell, Cobden and Bright but Palmerston swept all before him, achieving a Commons majority of 46. Roy Jenkins believes that this debate 'fortified Gladstone's hostility to Palmerston. Hitherto he had mildly disapproved of his character. Henceforward he deeply distrusted his policy' (see Further reading).

Gladstone had rather more success in the Commons when he attacked Palmerston's aggression towards China in the case of the *Arrow*, a Chinese ship arrested by the Chinese authorities for piracy in October 1856. The ship had been flying the British flag because it had been registered in Hong Kong. The Governor subsequently bombarded Canton when his demand for an apology was ignored. For Palmerston, this provided another opportunity to open more Chinese ports and extend the preferential trading agreements that the Opium War had brought. This time it was Cobden who introduced the censure motion. Gladstone spoke for a mere two hours denouncing Palmerston's 'defence of the indefensible' and pleading for a 'message of mercy and peace'. Certainly it must have contributed to Palmerston's defeat by 263 to 247 votes. But it was Palmerston who had better judged the mood of the electorate for, on dissolving parliament and calling a general election, he won with an increased majority. Cobden, Bright and other pacifists lost their seats and the war against China continued.

The Crimean War 1854–56

Gladstone tended to view the Crimean War from the perspective of the Chancellor of the Exchequer charged with financing it. Initially he supported British intervention and seemed more pro-war than the pacifist Aberdeen.

He [Aberdeen] said how could he bring himself to fight for the Turks? I replied we were not fighting for the Turks, but we were warning Russia off the forbidden ground ... the Emperor has invaded countries not his own, inflicted wrong on Turkey and ... most cruel wrong on the wretched inhabitants of the Principalities [Moldavia and Wallachia].

Gladstone hoped that British entry would bring the war to a speedier conclusion and he did not believe it would enlarge the conflict in any way. His views on the Eastern Question at this time were perhaps most clearly expressed in a speech he made in Manchester in October 1853 on the occasion of the unveiling of a statue to Peel. It was his first speech to a mass audience in the provinces in the impromptu style that would become his trademark. War had already broken out between Russia and Turkey but Britain had not yet entered the fray.

Gladstone adhered to the traditional British policy that the independence and integrity of the Turkish Empire should be maintained. He saw the dangers of an autocratic Russia expanding at Turkey's expense, but he also saw that the Turkish Empire was 'full of anomaly, full of misery and full of difficulty' in having sovereignty over millions of Christians. Even at this early stage, Gladstone spoke of the policy of peace and negotiation as the only basis of the 'real moral and social advancement of man'.

As the disasters of the war unfolded, and public demands for greater resources increased, Gladstone became more and more concerned about the cost. He had increased the income tax in March 1854, a few days before the formal declaration of war, and he was obliged to raise loans and indirect taxation as a matter of short-term expediency. He was more and more discomforted at having to abandon his Peelite financial principles and began to argue for an early peace settlement, claiming that as the Russians had withdrawn from Moldavia and Wallachia, the purpose of the war had been achieved. Once the Aberdeen Coalition fell (in February 1855), Gladstone argued that there was no longer any point in pursuing the siege of Sebastopol; it was wrong to try to punish Russia and impose a humiliating peace on her while the real cause of the trouble, the 'internal state or institutions of Turkey' were ignored. He also argued against a loan for Turkey as a subsidy to prop up 'the corrupt agents of a weak and uncertain government'. He found himself accused in the press of starving the war and, along with Cobden and Bright, he was branded as a traitor. There is no doubt that at this stage in his career Gladstone was extremely unpopular.

Foreign policy of the first ministry

Before he became Prime Minister, Gladstone's direct involvement in foreign policy was scanty. His spell as Colonial Secretary (1845–46) lasted barely six months, and in those days his callow view was that colonisation was one of the 'best means of advancing and diffusing civilisation' and 'the creation of so many happy Englands'. Although Gladstone was in the cabinet at the start of the Crimean War and during the American Civil War, most events were seen through the eyes of the

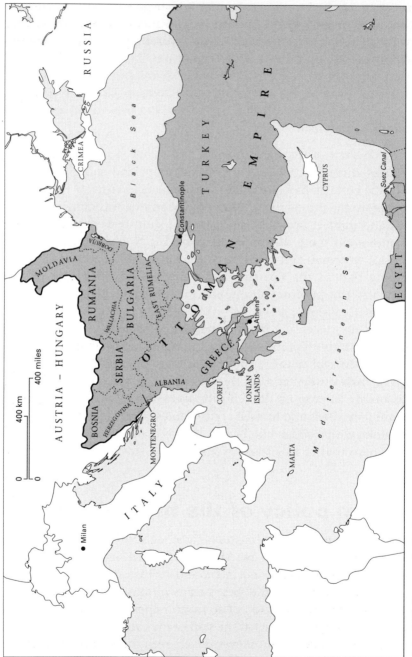

Figure 5 The Ottoman or Turkish Empire

Chancellor of the Exchequer. As such he shared responsibility for the Anglo-French Trade agreement of 1860 and certainly saw free trade as the means of bringing about peace and understanding between nations (see Chapter 1).

Franco-Prussian War 1870–71

The first major crisis in foreign affairs to claim Gladstone's attention as Prime Minister was the Franco-Prussian War. As a signatory to the Treaty of London which had established Belgian independence, Britain was clearly an interested party and Gladstone was far from being an isolationist, like more radical Liberals such as John Bright. Believing that 'the nations of Europe are a family', Gladstone, according to Professor Matthew, saw British involvement in the quarrel as wholly natural: England's 'hand will not be unready to be lifted up, on every fit and hopeful occasion, in sustaining the general sense of Europe against a disturber of the public peace' (see Further reading). In this respect, and in his view of the national interest, Gladstone was following in the footsteps of Castlereagh and Canning.

Despite an initial Prussian sympathy among the public, at the outset of the war Britain maintained a strictly neutral position. Indeed Gladstone said: 'On the face of the facts France is wrong, but as to the personal trustworthiness the two moving spirits on the respective sides, Napoleon and Bismarck, are nearly on a par.' He was determined to keep Britain out of the war, to ensure the safety of Belgium but to avoid any large increase in Britain's military strength. Nevertheless, Gladstone asked the War Office to 'study the means of sending 20,000 men to Antwerp' should Belgium's neutrality need defending. In the event he was able to persuade each of the combatants to sign a treaty with Britain whereby if either one of them violated the neutrality of Belgium, Britain would cooperate with the other in its defence.

Once Prussia had won the war, Gladstone switched his concern to the annexation of Alsace-Lorraine which he deplored, not as Palmerston might have done, because it threatened the balance of power in Europe, but as a return to the 'old and cruel practice of treating the population of a civilised European country as mere chattels'. Here we have another example of his faith in the Concert of Europe because he wanted to rally the neutral powers of Europe against this annexation.

He was unable to persuade the cabinet to support him, however, and the idea was dropped.

The *Alabama* Arbitration 1872

No event in Gladstone's first ministry, and perhaps no other in his entire career, reveals more clearly his concern for morality and justice in foreign affairs than his handling of the *Alabama* dispute. This had been rumbling on ever since the Birkenhead-built, southern-owned ship had slipped out of the Mersey in 1862 to start a two-year campaign of severe damage to northern merchant shipping in the American Civil War. The northern states claimed, with some justification, that this contravened Britain's declared neutral status and so demanded compensation for the damage done. Palmerston and Russell refused to accept any responsibility on behalf of the British government and as time went by the claims became ever more extravagant. Not only had the *Alabama* damaged shipping but it had, according to the United States, been responsible for prolonging the war. In 1868 Disraeli's government expressed its willingness to take the case to arbitration but it was Gladstone's foreign secretary, Granville, who represented Britain at the international arbitration conference at Geneva where the sum of £3¼ million was finally agreed. Although only a third of the figure demanded by the United States, the verdict of public opinion was that it was too large. Roy Jenkins has calculated that, after comparison with the national income at the time, it would be about £150 billion today (see Further reading). This led to a steady improvement in Anglo-American relations but Gladstone's foreign policy was widely perceived to be weak. His government became more unpopular and it was a contributory factor in its defeat.

Ashanti War 1873–74

It is surprising that Gladstone, who was so warm in support of self-government, should have been responsible for the extension of British colonies in Africa. In the case of the Gold Coast there seems to have been almost a 'forward policy' of the kind Gladstone was critical of when pursued by Disraeli. The war was precipitated by two events: the acquisition by Britain of some forts on the Gold Coast from the Dutch and the accession to the throne by the warlike King Kofi-Kari. His people, the Ashantis, had already attacked British settlements, in 1824, and proceeded to use the skull of the murdered British governor as a royal drinking cup. Increased British activity against the slave trade particularly annoyed King Kofi because this was the main source of his wealth. He proceeded to invade the British protected area in 1873, advancing within 12 miles of the chief British base at Cape Coast Castle. Gladstone was reluctantly persuaded by the combined efforts of the Colonial Office and the War Office that a military expedition was needed. Indeed such was the speed with which the select force under Sir Garnet Wolseley was collected and despatched that the expedition was on its way before the cabinet met. Gladstone was pleased that it turned out to be quick, cheap and successful: the Ashanti were defeated, their capital occupied and King Kofi's palace destroyed. Though by the time peace was made Disraeli was in power, all the key decisions were made by the Gladstone administration.

Opposition to 'Beaconsfieldism'

It was concern about foreign affairs that brought Gladstone out of retirement in 1876 to criticise Disraeli's handling of the Eastern Question. The weakness of the Turkish Empire, the incompetence and corruption of its government and the inability of the Sultan to control the many distant and disparate parts of his lands was not by any means a new problem for Europe. The traditional British view was that the Empire should be kept together because the consequences of disintegration or partition, with the likely subsequent extension of Russian power, would be worse. As Castlereagh once famously said to the Tsar of Russia: 'Barbarous as it is, Turkey forms in the system of Europe, a necessary evil.' It was no secret that Russia wanted a warm-water port which it could use all year round and that Constantinople would suit her purpose very well. Successive British foreign ministers feared that the extension of Russian influence into the eastern Mediterranean would be a threat to the British route to India. During the nineteenth century, with liberal and nationalist movements sweeping Europe, various ethnic groups began to seek either freedom from Turkey, self-government, or in some cases, complete independence. In these circumstances, British policy became less plain, for public opinion tended to favour nationalist Christian groups struggling for freedom against the autocratic Muslim Turks. This was the case for instance in the 1820s when the Greeks were fighting for independence.

The Treaty of Paris, which had ended the Crimean War in 1856, proved no long-term solution to the problems of the Turkish Empire.

In 1870, taking advantage of Europe's preoccupation with the Franco-Prussian War, Russia unilaterally broke the Black Sea clause and sailed her warships out there; Turkey ignored promises to treat her Christian subjects reasonably: indeed they were treated as serfs. Conflict began again in 1875 when a rebellion, starting in Bosnia and Herzegovina, spread to Serbia, Montenegro and Bulgaria. Disraeli was suspicious of Russian intentions and had no particular sympathy for the Baltic Christians. On the contrary, the experiences he had enjoyed during his 'grand tour', when he spent many months during 1830–31 in the Turkish Empire, including six weeks in Constantinople, left him with a fascination and admiration for all things Turkish and Muslim. Thus Disraeli did not join with the other European powers in the Berlin Memorandum demanding that Turkey institute a prompt reform programme. Consequently, Turkey believed she had Britain's support and far from instituting reforms, proceeded to make even greater efforts to crush the rebels, in the course of which monstrous atrocities were committed.

For Gladstone the issues were perfectly clear: great crimes had been perpetrated by infidels on innocent Christians. He took up his pen and in four days wrote his most famous pamphlet, *The Bulgarian Horrors and the Question of the East*. He made his case vigorously and in colourful language:

We now know in detail that there have been perpetrated ... crimes and outrages so vast in scale as to exceed all modern example, and so utterly vile and so fierce in character, that it passes the power of heart to conceive, and of tongue and pen adequately to describe them. These are the Bulgarian horrors ... the violent lawlessness which still stalks over the land ... murdering, burning, impaling, roasting men and women and children indiscriminately ...

The matter has become too painfully real for us to be scared by the hobgoblin of Russia ... Let the Turks now carry away their abuses in the only possible manner, namely by carrying off themselves ... one and all, bag and baggage ... There is not a criminal in a European jail, there is not a cannibal in the South Sea Islands, whose indignation would not arise and overboil at the recital of that which has been done.

Gladstone made a rare visit to his Greenwich constituency and made a great speech in the rain on Blackheath to about 10,000 people. This was the first of many speeches up and down the country and his pamphlet became a bestseller, soon to be followed by another and numerous letters and articles in the press.

Gladstone thus revived his duel with Disraeli. For his part, the latter was dismissive of Gladstone's pamphlet which he described as 'vindictive and ill written ... of all the Bulgarian horrors, perhaps the greatest'. He maintained that in defending the integrity of Turkey he was protecting British interests and in particular the 'Empire of England'. Government popularity was restored by Disraeli's success at the Conference of Berlin, and Gladstone became correspondingly unpopular. But then defeats in South Africa and Afghanistan brought further opportunities to criticise Disraeli's foreign policies, culminating in the Midlothian Campaign.

The principles in practice

'The blessings of peace?' Afghanistan and South Africa

Gladstone entered upon his second ministry with the express purpose of reversing 'Beaconsfieldism': those policies of Disraeli's which he had criticised so much in opposition. This proved more difficult in practice than he had expected. Gladstone had no intention of increasing Britain's imperial responsibilities but found himself drawn into situations where this seemed to be the inevitable outcome. Nor was balancing the 'equal rights of all nations' a simple matter.

The new government inherited two continuing problems as a direct result of Disraeli's imperial policy: in Afghanistan and the Transvaal. Conservative policy proved most easily reversible in Afghanistan. This country was regarded as a buffer state where British influence was vital in keeping Russia out of India. The 'forward policy' of Disraeli and his viceroy of India, Lord Lytton, had led to a war, apparently successful for the British, but in September 1879 the entire British mission in Kabul was slaughtered by Afghan rebels resenting the extension of British influence and civil war broke out. Disraeli therefore authorised further military action to restore order. During his Midlothian Campaign Gladstone had been highly critical of the Conservative government's policy in Afghanistan but now, since the fall of Disraeli's

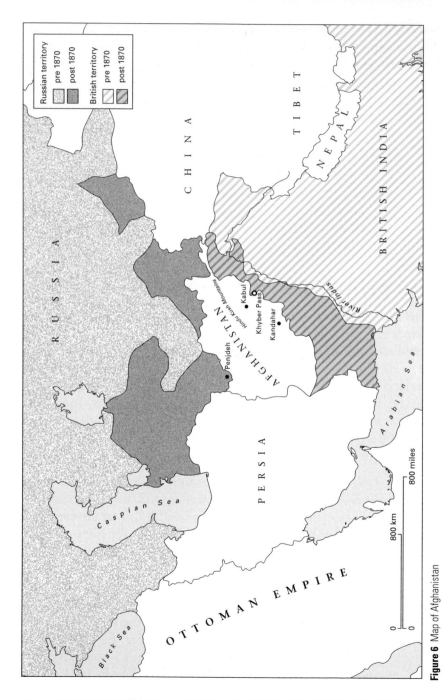

Figure 6 Map of Afghanistan

government in April 1880, it was his responsibility to resolve the matter. General Roberts was authorised to march from Kabul to Kandahar to put down the insurrection. He did this with speed and efficiency, thus allowing Gladstone to reverse the 'forward policy' of the previous administration by withdrawing British troops from Afghanistan, but from a position of strength. Despite the fact that the new ruler remained friendly to Britain and Russia stayed out of Afghanistan (apart from Penjdeh) for the next 20 years, the Conservatives pointed to the British withdrawal from Afghanistan as typical of the weakness of Liberal foreign policy.

Disraeli's legacy in the Transvaal proved less easy to settle satisfactorily. The problem here was that Gladstone had raised the expectations of the Boers during the Midlothian Campaign by referring to the annexation of the Transvaal as 'insane'. Back in office, however, on the advice of the Colonial Office, he began to think of federation as the answer to the problems of South Africa as a whole. This fitted well with his ideas of self-governing colonies existing contentedly under the guidance of the mother country. Thus there was no immediate withdrawal from the Transvaal. Disappointment among the Boers turned to anger and rebellion. Gladstone, enmeshed in the problems of Ireland and the Exchequer, relied on the advice of his agents on the ground. Despite instructions from London to work for peace, Sir George Colley, the Governor of Natal, set out to crush the rebellion, only to be defeated at Laing's Nek in January 1881 and the following month more comprehensively at Majuba Hill where he was killed. At home there was a clamour for revenge and the cabinet was divided, but for Gladstone now the issues were clear: it was neither morally nor economically right to pursue the Boers to ultimate defeat. The Convention of Pretoria in August 1881 recognised the Transvaal's independence 'subject to the **suzerainty** of her Majesty' and British control of her foreign policy. The terms were amended three years later by the London Convention when the term 'suzerainty' was omitted. The Boers took Gladstone's actions to be symptomatic of weakness, as did large numbers of people at home. Affairs in Afghanistan and Southern Africa paled into insignificance however, when compared with the more traumatic events in Egypt and the Sudan.

KEY TERM

Suzerainty means sovereignty, the position of one state exercising power over a dependent state, usually by controlling its foreign affairs.

The reluctant Imperialist? Occupation of Egypt 1882

It is most particularly in his dealings with Egypt that Gladstone stands accused of abandoning his right principles of foreign policy. From all that he had said and written to date one would expect Gladstone to have been sympathetic to the Egyptian nationalist movement and certainly not likely to implement a 'forward policy' of the kind he criticised when carried out by Palmerston or Disraeli. Yet he seemed drawn into an uncharacteristic policy by the force of circumstances.

British interest in Egypt had grown since the opening of the Suez Canal in 1869 and was further increased by Disraeli's purchase of 45% of the shares in 1875. The Canal was especially useful for the new freight-carrying steamships and by 1882 it was taking more than five million tons of shipping and 80% of that was British. Britain had an additional financial interest in Egypt for both banks and individuals had lent substantial sums of money to the Khedive Ismail. Though it was still nominally part of the Turkish Empire, the Sultan lacked the ability and the resources to assume control of Egypt's problems. The country's finances were therefore placed under the Dual Control of Britain and France and this was the situation when Gladstone returned to office. It was soon to change for a nationalist uprising, fuelled by resentment against foreigners and the wretched living conditions of many peasants, swept through the country led by an Egyptian army officer, Arabi Pasha. In June 1882 rioting in Alexandria led to the deaths of some 50 Europeans and injuries to 60 more.

When public opinion turned against 'Egypt for the Egyptians' in favour of 'order', and Gladstone realised there was no chance of action from the Sultan, he still hoped for European action and a conference was held at Constantinople to investigate this. With Germany unwilling and France cautious, Gladstone now found himself virtually isolated in a cabinet demanding British intervention. Exhausted from long sittings in the Commons over Ireland, he was persuaded to send Arabi an ultimatum: if he did not stop fortifying Alexandria the British Navy would bombard it. This happened on 11 July 1882. It was the beginning of a full-scale operation. Sir Garnet Wolseley was sent to Egypt with 25,000 men who gained a complete victory over Arabi's army at Tel-el-Kebir with few casualties on the British side. Gladstone was pleased at the efficiency of the post-Cardwell Army and the victory made him popular, but he did not intend the British Army to remain in Egypt. However 'order' now seemed dependent on British forces and he could see that the Suez Canal must inevitably be safer with the presence of British troops than without them and as long as Britain held India, the safety of the Canal was paramount. This was how Egypt came to be, unofficially, part of the British Empire, although Gladstone insisted that the occupation was only temporary until the country's finances were regularised. When a conference of the powers convened in London for this very purpose failed to agree in 1884, the withdrawal of British troops became more distant, but by then Gladstone was embroiled in troubles over the Sudan.

Murderer of Gordon? Debacle in the Sudan 1884–85

The occupation of Egypt led to British involvement in the Sudan which had been ruled by Egypt for 60 years. Its people were poor and wretched so that when a leader emerged in 1883, calling himself the 'Mahdi', or Messiah, he had no shortage of followers. His army rapidly swept all before it. For Egypt, the prudent decision would have been to let at least the southern part of Sudan go, but perhaps humiliated by the British occupation, the Khedive sent an army, led by British officers commanded by General Hicks, to subdue the Mahdists. Gladstone's sympathies were with the Mahdists. He said, 'these people are struggling to be free; and they are struggling rightly to be free': he had no wish to see Britain involved.

In November, however, Hicks and his army were massacred by the Mahdists. Though Gladstone still favoured withdrawal, it was clear that this would not be a simple matter. There were still Egyptian garrisons in the Sudan commanded by British officers and there were civilians who needed protection. The cabinet decided on evacuation in January and Gladstone returned to Hawarden leaving the details to his ministers. In his absence Granville, Hartington and Northbrook took the decision to allow General Charles Gordon to go to the Sudan to

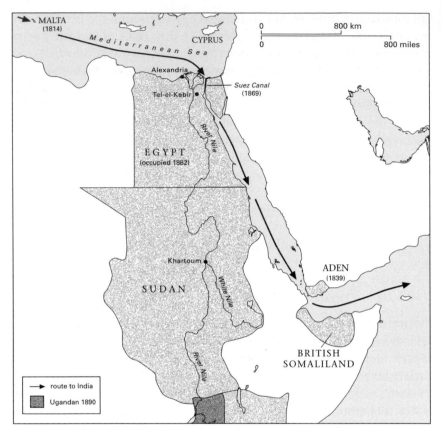

Figure 7 Egypt and the Sudan

supervise the withdrawal. Unfortunately he was not the man to organise a retreat, any more than he was prepared to follow instructions or listen to advice. Once in Khartoum, the Sudanese capital, he decided the Mahdists could and should be crushed. Instead of organising the retreat, he asked for more troops which the government refused to send. By the end of March he was besieged in Khartoum.

At home the press was orchestrating public opinion to demand help be sent. The government prevaricated all summer, debating whether to send an expedition to rescue Gordon who, after all, had disobeyed instructions, what size of relief force would be appropriate, what route it should take. Finally action was decided on and Wolseley was sent up the Nile on a rescue mission, only to reach Khartoum two days after it had fallen to the Mahdi and Gordon killed. A national hero now became a martyr. The government became extremely unpopular and the Prime Minister especially so. From being the GOM, the Grand Old Man, Gladstone was devastatingly translated by opponents into the MOG, Murderer of Gordon. The Queen exactly expressed the public mood when she sent an angry telegram to Gladstone: 'These news from Khartoum are frightful, and to think that all this might have been prevented and many precious lives saved by earlier action is too fearful.' In the Commons the government's majority fell to 14 on a censure motion. Far from avenging the death of Gordon as many were demanding, Gladstone compounded his unpopularity by withdrawing from the Sudan.

How successful was Gladstone's foreign policy?

Certainly Gladstone seemed increasingly to lack the sure touch and identification with the public mood which he had earlier enjoyed. Perhaps this is partly because in this second ministry, foreign affairs moved beyond Europe to areas about which Gladstone was less in-formed and perhaps less interested and less sympathetic – areas where he was dependent on the advice of subordinates. Opponents at the time accused Gladstone of inconsistency, even hypocrisy in the con-duct of foreign policy. While it would be an exaggeration to say that the principles defined in the Midlothian Campaign were merely elec-tion rhetoric, in office Gladstone was forced to consider British inter-ests rather more than he had anticipated. Roy Jenkins says: 'Gladstone was constantly compromising between imperialist pressures and his own instincts, which were a mixture of Little Englander caution and Concert of Europe idealism. Neither pointed to the expansion of terri-tory or colonial wars.' (See Further reading.) Radicals and Noncon-formists among his supporters regarded the occupation of Egypt as a betrayal. John Bright resigned from the cabinet in protest, yet it is difficult to see what else Gladstone could have done once he had accepted the economic and strategic arguments. He can be accused justifiably of indecision on occasion, but then Gladstone had other, more pressing problems to deal with nearer home.

Essay writing

An essay is essentially an extended *argument*, written in direct response to a specific question.

Planning the essay

Consider these points first:

1 *What is the question really asking?*
2 *What does it cover?* Work out what you need to know.
3 *Do you know enough about it?* Read through class notes and handouts first, noting points that are relevant to the question and identifying areas where you need more information or ideas. Read some of the books and/or articles from your reading list (see page 126) and start making notes as outlined in Chapter 1.
4 *How much research should you do?* Try to look at a good range of material to get a full picture. For A-Level purposes you *must* read beyond the textbook, but be *selective*. You don't necessarily need to read a whole book, or note down information you already have from other sources.
5 *What do you think?* Now sit back and think about what the question is asking. Try to work out what, on balance, your answer is. Try to write it down in *one* sentence.
6 *Why do you think that?* List the evidence you would need to support your view.
7 *But – !* Now try to knock your argument down. What objections are there? What have you conveniently ignored? What other interpretations are there of the evidence you have gathered?
8 *Now what do you think?* Perhaps you have changed your mind. What do you think is the most convincing answer to the question?

Consider the question, 'How far did Gladstone implement his "right principles" of foreign policy?' Go through the stages above.

Writing the essay

The introduction
This must link *directly* with the question, be fairly brief – and interesting!

The main body of the essay – your argument
Write in paragraphs. Your essay is likely to be clearer if each one deals

with a separate point in your argument. Remember A B C – accuracy, brevity, clarity.

Always support your ideas with evidence, but select this for its relevance to the question. Don't pile up too much information. Avoid telling the reader all you know about the subject.

Write in your own words unless you are actually quoting.

An essay is a formal piece of writing. Take care with spelling and punctuation, avoid slang abbreviations and note forms.

The conclusion
This should be brief. Sum up, state clearly your main idea, argument or explanation. It's your last chance to leave the reader with a favourable impression!

CHAPTER FIVE

GLADSTONE AND IRELAND

Objectives
◢ To understand why Ireland needed pacifying in 1868
◢ To consider how successful Gladstone was in his mission to pacify Ireland
◢ To see how Gladstone decided on Home Rule for Ireland and how he tried to achieve it.

'My mission is to pacify Ireland'

The story of Gladstone receiving the telegram inviting him to Windsor Castle following the Liberal election victory in 1868 is a well-known one. According to Evelyn Ashley, Palmerston's former secretary, who was staying at Hawarden at the time, Gladstone was enjoying his favourite relaxation of tree felling when the telegram arrived. He put his axe down to read it and commented 'very significant'. Then after returning to his task for a few minutes he said: 'My mission is to pacify Ireland.' It seems a rather curious remark for Gladstone to make because he had not previously shown much interest in Ireland and such interest as he had shown did not indicate much sympathy for the Irish and their problems. In 1845 he resigned from the cabinet over Peel's proposal to increase the government grant to Maynooth College, where priests were trained for the Catholic Church in Ireland. As Chancellor of the Exchequer he introduced the income tax to Ireland in 1853. Indeed he tended to regard Ireland as a potential drain on resources. In 1859 he wrote to his wife that 'all the Irish were there (in the House of Commons) vying with each other in eagerness to plunder the public purse'. Though widely travelled, Ireland had never featured on any of Gladstone's itineraries. His remark thus raises two interesting questions: what prompted his concern for Ireland at this particular time and why did it need pacifying?

Part of the answer to the first question lies in the Fenian activity which brought Ireland to the notice of the British public in 1867. In an incident in Manchester, a policeman was killed as an armed gang rescued two Fenian prisoners, and in London 12 innocent people lost their lives when part of the wall of Clerkenwell prison was blown up during the attempted rescue of two more Fenians. While he condemned the outrages Gladstone acknowledged that the Irish suffered genuine grievances. A few days later he made a speech in Southport, Lancashire where he mentioned the need for both Irish Church and Irish land reform but without making specific proposals. It is more likely, however, that the Fenian outrages were merely the catalyst which brought to a head policies which were already approaching maturity.

Gladstone also now realised that here he had an issue which could unite the Liberals after their divisions over parliamentary reform. Just before leaving office Russell had written a pamphlet advocating the dis-establishment of the Irish Church so Whig support for such a measure was likely. Radicals and Nonconformists favoured dis-establishment as a matter of principle. Gladstone made Irish Church reform a key issue in the election campaign. In October he made his famous speech likening the Protestant ascendancy in Ireland to the upas tree, a tree so poisonous that it was said to kill all life around it:

... and now at length the day has come when, as we hope, the axe has been laid at the root of the tree, and it nods and quivers from its root to its base. It wants, Gentlemen, one stroke more, the stroke of these elections.

Why did Ireland need pacifying in 1868?

Ireland had long been a problem for English governments. It was initially seen as a place of strategic importance to an enemy power, probably Catholic, wanting to use it as a base from which to invade the mainland. For this reason it was seen as important for England to control the island. By 1868 there was considerable unrest in Ireland for a number of reasons.

◢ A sense of separate Irish nationhood had been growing at least since the 1790s. It had been increased by what many Irish saw as an imposed political union in 1801. This led to Ireland being governed by an English Viceroy and an English dominated administration at Dublin Castle which applied English law made at Westminster by a parliament in which there were a 100 MPs representing Irish constituencies.

◢ The Irish population was largely Roman Catholic (5.3 million out of a population of just under 6 million according to the 1861 Census). The State Church, however, though called the Church of Ireland, was the Protestant Anglican Church and the Irish bitterly resented having to pay taxes for the upkeep of churches which they never attended, as well as having to support their own churches and priests.

◢ Most of the land was owned by wealthy English who did not live in Ireland and saw their Irish estates merely as a source of income. The Irish population had grown rapidly in the first half of the nineteenth century and there was very little industry except in the Protestant north-east corner of Ulster. By 1841 about eight million people were living in conditions of dire poverty. Blame for the disastrous famine of 1845–47, when hundreds of thousands of people died of starvation, was widely laid at the door of the Westminster government which had sent inappropriate help – much too little and too late. Irish emigrants to America promoted the famine as the most powerful nationalist symbol of all and were prolific fundraisers for the cause. The Fenians were founded in Ireland and the United States in 1858 to campaign for an independent Irish republic.

How did Gladstone try to pacify Ireland in his first ministry?

Gladstone set to work immediately on his Irish Church Bill. He was personally involved in its drafting and introduced it himself in the Commons. He took the leading role in all the debates and clearly demonstrated his mastery of the minutest details. It passed the Commons with the large majority of 114 and in the light of this, the Lords hesitated to provoke a constitutional crisis so soon in the parliament by rejecting it.

The main terms of the Irish Church Act and the First Irish Land Act are set out below.

Irish Church Act 1869

◢ The Anglican Church in Ireland was dis-established (i.e. it was no longer the official State religion, Catholics were no longer obliged to pay tithes for its upkeep and the Irish Anglican bishops and archbishops lost their right to sit in the Lords).
◢ The Church's property (valued at £16 million) was shared between pensions for the clergy and compensation for their loss of office (£10 million) and relief of poverty and education in Ireland.
◢ The State grant to Maynooth College was abolished.
◢ Tenants of Church lands were allowed to buy their farms (about 6,000 did).

First Irish Land Act 1870

◢ The Ulster custom of 'tenant-right' was recognised in law. (This right ensured that tenants could not be evicted as long as they kept up with their rent.)
◢ Unprotected tenants (i.e. in the rest of Ireland) who were· evicted were to be compensated by the landlord according to a scale of damages based on the size of the holding.
◢ All evicted tenants, including those who had failed to pay rent, would be entitled to compensation for improvements they had made to their holdings.
◢ Loans of public money, up to two-thirds of the purchase price, could be advanced to tenants who wished to buy their holdings (John Bright clause).

Irish Universities Bill 1873

Gladstone's proposal was to combine the Queen's University with its 'godless' colleges at Cork and Belfast set up by Peel, with Trinity College, Dublin (and the privately endowed Catholic college in Dublin and the Presbyterian Magee college, if they wished to join) into a new University of Dublin. In order to avoid religious difficulties, theology, philosophy and modern history were to be excluded from the curriculum. Gladstone regarded this measure as the first step towards a general plan for Irish education but he did not have the full support of his cabinet colleagues. Hartington, Irish Secretary since December 1870, believed there were two matters more deserving of legislation than university education: Irish railways and local government. Neither was there significant support for the measure among MPs. Irish bishops were completely opposed to integrated education. Thus despite Gladstone's persuasive speeches in the Commons, the Bill was defeated by three votes. Gladstone decided to resign rather than dissolve parliament for there was little prospect of a Liberal victory if a general election were to be held. Disraeli's refusal to lead a minority government forced him to carry on.

How successful were these measures?

Gladstone was pleased with his first government's measures for Ireland. In 1871 he said, 'There is nothing that Ireland has asked and which this country and this parliament have refused', although he qualified this by admitting that the single grievance of Irish university education was yet to be solved. He was probably right to regard the Irish Church Act as successful for it did remove the main religious grievance of the Catholics, though it made little difference to the lives of most Irish people. By contrast, his satisfaction with the Land Act seems somewhat optimistic. It proved difficult to determine exactly where the 'Ulster custom' existed; tenants continued to be evicted because there was nothing to prevent a landlord from raising rents so high that the tenant was unable to pay; little use was made of John Bright's clause because few tenants could raise even the third of the price needed to pay for their holdings. But Gladstone failed in another sense. He had wanted to demonstrate to the Irish the Westminster parliament's ability to legislate to solve their legitimate grievances. He thought this would bring social and political stability within the union: peace would reign and the Irish would abandon Fenianism. This did not happen. Gladstone actually raised Irish expectations which he did not meet. Irish tenants wanted the 'Three Fs' (fixity of tenure, freedom of sale and fair rents) which his measure failed to provide.

To be fair to Gladstone it has to be said that the 1870 Land Act went against the most deeply held nineteenth-century beliefs about the rights of property owners. It introduced what was to many Liberals an unparalleled degree of government interference in the relations between landlords and tenants, and was regarded as a very dangerous precedent. Whigs in Gladstone's own cabinet, such as Clarendon and Argyll, saw it as an outright attack on property which could spread to England. The legacy of Gladstone's legislation was discontent in Ireland which could not be quelled by the release of Fenian prisoners or Coercion Acts. By-elections began to bring successes for the infant Home Rule movement but Gladstone failed to recognise the significance of this for the Liberal Party in Ireland and remained optimistic, even complacent, about the situation there.

Second ministry reforms 1880–85

Before returning to office Gladstone made his only visit to Ireland. (Stepping ashore from a cruise ship to attend a church service in 1880 hardly counts as a visit.) In mid October 1877 he went to Dublin and stayed almost a month, visiting also Wicklow and Kildare, the counties immediately adjacent to the capital. He admired the scenery at Glendalough, but can have gained few insights about the realities of life in Ireland staying as he did in the great houses of the aristocracy. Certainly he seemed unaware of the approaching agricultural crisis.

Unlike 1868, Ireland was hardly mentioned in the 1880 election campaign and Gladstone did not begin his second ministry with a pre-planned legislative programme. As we saw in Chapter 4, his intention was to remain in office just long enough to reverse the worst aspects of Beaconsfieldism and then retire. Events in Ireland, however, forced his hand. The situation there was now very different from that of Gladstone's first ministry. The agricultural depression of the late 1870s was devastating for Ireland. Faced with diminishing profits, landlords raised rents and evicted those who could not pay. Between 1877 and 1880 evictions increased five-fold and conditions for the peasants were worse than at any time since the famine. A second difference was the existence of a separate Home Rule Party of 61 members at Westminster, now led by the charismatic Charles Stuart Parnell who had made his uncompromising view clear in his maiden speech when he asked: 'Why should Ireland be treated as a geographical fragment of England? Ireland is not a geographical fragment. She is a nation.' From Gladstone's perspective there was another difference: his second cabinet was far more divided, even in its early days. This was to make the passage of legislation for Ireland more difficult. Agrarian distress, the doubling of evictions in the first six months of the year together with the activities of the Land League and especially the violence (1879–82 was known as the Land War), brought Ireland to the top of the political agenda within eight weeks of the government taking office.

The government's first response was to introduce a Compensation for Disturbance Bill which was intended to provide compensation for an evicted tenant, provided he could prove to the courts that he had a good reason for failing to pay his rent, that he was willing to continue his tenancy on reasonable terms and that these terms had been rejected by his landlord. This proposal was overwhelmingly defeated in the Lords in August. The Irish Secretary, W. E. Forster, began to see the way to peace in Ireland in terms of coercion but Gladstone was against this route. Already in June he had set up the Bessborough Commission to enquire into the workings of the 1870 Land Act and in October he put his ideas together in a paper entitled 'Obstruction and Devolution'. He said: 'Devolution may supply the means of partially meeting and satisfying, at least so far as is legitimate, another call. I refer to the call for what is called ... Home Rule.' But in the cabinet only Chamberlain and Bright showed any interest in his proposals. Nevertheless it indicates the direction Gladstone's mind was taking. Meanwhile the Land League began its famous boycotting campaign and there were many unofficial outrages. Ireland seemed near revolution. When, at the turn of the year, Bessborough reported in favour of the 'three Fs', Gladstone decided on a further Land Act but could only secure the support of the cabinet if it was preceded by coercion.

Coercion Act 1881
This suspended habeas corpus, thus allowing suspects to be jailed without trial. The Irish Party, led by Parnell, used their obstruction tactics to hold up the Bill, keeping the House sitting continuously for 41 hours, prompting the Speaker to introduce the device of the **'Guillotine'**. The government promptly took advantage of the new Act to arrest and imprison Michael Davitt, the leader of the Land League.

KEY TERM

In this context **Guillotine** means a motion to curtail debate on a Bill, usually proposed by the minister responsible. It sets a time limit for debate on each clause of the Bill, usually at the committee stage of its passage through parliament. It is used by the government of the day either to hasten the passage of a contentious Bill, or to ensure a Bill does not run out of time, for if a Bill has not completed all its stages before the end of the parliamentary session it is lost and has to be reintroduced next session.

Second Irish Land Act 1881

This granted the 'three Fs' demanded by the Land League.

◢ Fair rents: an Irish Land Commission, with the status of a High Court, was created with powers to decide on rents which were then fixed for 15 years.

◢ Fixity of tenure: a tenant could not be evicted as long as he paid his rent.

◢ Free sale: a tenant could sell his lease, without his landlord's permission, to anyone who would give him a fair price for it. Thus he could recover the costs of any improvements he had made.

◢ The State would now advance three-quarters of the purchase price to a tenant wishing to buy his holding.

◢ Tenants who were in arrears were excluded from the provisions of the Act.

The long struggle for the Bill through the committee stage acted as a stimulus in keeping the Liberal Party together, but it did not bring peace to Ireland. Many in the Land League argued that it did nothing for those tenants who were in arrears and therefore still liable to be evicted. The more extreme contended that rent should never be paid to foreign (English) landlords and that it was the violence which had gained these concessions and therefore it should be continued to obtain more. In a speech at Leeds Gladstone warned Parnell and the Land League: 'If it shall appear that there is still to be fought a final conflict in Ireland between law on the one side and sheer lawlessness on the other, ... then I say, without hesitation, the resources of civilisation against its enemies are not yet exhausted.' In reply Parnell attacked Gladstone as 'this masquerading knight errant, this pretending champion of the rights of every nation except those of the Irish nation'. Within the week Parnell was arrested on the recommendation of Forster and imprisoned in Dublin's Kilmainham Jail.

The Land League's retort was to call a rent strike and the government then declared the League illegal. This shows that although Gladstone was opposed to coercion in principle he was prepared to use it when he saw a clear advantage. In this case he wanted to give the Land Act a chance to work. He believed (rightly) that there were many Irish tenants anxious to use the Land Commission to reduce their rents. It is remarkable that despite the setbacks, all the other difficulties of his second ministry and his increasing age, Gladstone retained that optimism that was so characteristic of his brand of Liberalism. He wrote to Forster:

If Ireland is still divided between Orangemen and law-haters, then our task is hopeless: but our belief and contention always is that a more intelligent and less impassioned body has gradually come to exist in Ireland. It is on this body, its precepts and examples, that our hopes depend, for if we are at war with a nation we cannot win.

The Kilmainham Treaty 1882
Parnell's imprisonment provided him with an opportunity for reflection and he believed his power and influence would diminish if he remained there. Gladstone, for his part, thought that Parnell could be more use out of jail if he would employ his influence to curb such crime and violence as still existed. An agreement was reached whereby Parnell would be released and the government would introduce an Arrears Bill to help the 100,000 tenants who owed such large sums of rent that they were excluded from the Land Act. Parnell insisted public money would be needed for this purpose. In return he would accept the Land Act and use his influence to end the violence. Forster, who wanted to continue a policy of coercion, resigned the day after Parnell's release.

The Phoenix Park murders 1882
In Forster's place Gladstone appointed Lord Frederick Cavendish, Hartington's younger brother. As the husband of his wife's favourite niece, Lucy Lyttleton, he was more like a son-in-law to Gladstone.

Within hours of arriving in Dublin, while strolling in Phoenix Park with Thomas Burke, the Irish Under-Secretary, the pair were set upon and hacked to death by a gang of assassins wielding surgical knives. This was a devastating blow to Gladstone personally, but it was to have profound consequences for the future of Ireland. In England there was a sense of shock and outrage and 50,000 people attended Cavendish's funeral at Chatsworth. There was a strong public demand for more coercion which Gladstone was obliged to concede and powers to arrest on suspicion allowed the Royal Irish Constabulary to track down the murderers, members of a secret society, the Irish National Invincibles.

But Gladstone was determined not to be deflected by the tragedy and he began to correspond with Parnell via his mistress, Katherine O'Shea. This was not as strange a move as it might seem because she belonged to an eminent Liberal family: her uncle, Lord Hatherley, was Gladstone's first Lord Chancellor and her brother was Sir Evelyn Wood, whose diplomacy after Majuba Hill had led to the Convention of Pretoria with the Boers the year before. Katherine was a skilled negotiator herself and through her mediation Gladstone and Parnell enjoyed some three years of cooperation. The Arrears Bill was passed and though it fell short of the demands of some, Ireland experienced a period of relative calm. Gladstone was occupied with foreign affairs and parliamentary reform. LORD RANDOLPH CHURCHILL on behalf of the Tories began to woo Parnell, indicating that if his followers voted for them, they would not renew the Coercion Act. Thus Gladstone's government fell on 8 June 1885, when the Irish Party voted with the Tories on an amendment to the Budget and 76 Liberals abstained. Unlike Disraeli in 1873, Salisbury was prepared to undertake a minority government.

Profile LORD RANDOLPH CHURCHILL (1849–94)

Third son of the Duke of Marlborough, educated at Eton and Merton College, Oxford; Conservative MP for Woodstock, 1874; became leader of 'Fourth Party', group within Conservative Party seeking to secure working-class vote through social reform; Secretary for India in Salisbury's ministry (1885–86); Chancellor of the Exchequer and Leader of the Commons 1886 in Salisbury's second ministry but resigned within five months when some cabinet colleagues opposed his proposed cuts to the armed forces budget.

The road to Home Rule

By the end of 1885 Gladstone seemed to have reached the conclusion that the introduction of some kind of Home Rule was the only way to settle the problems of Ireland. This was no road to Damascus conversion, more the inevitable conclusion, gradually reached, based on ideas and principles he had long held and his response to recent events in Ireland. Gladstone always maintained that Home Rule involved no change of mind.

The starting point for Gladstone was that he had long regarded the Act of Union as 'a gigantic though excusable mistake', caused by the war with France. Out of office he did much reading about Ireland, especially its history. He became convinced of the reality of Irish nationality. If the Irish were a nation, they were as entitled to self government as the Bulgarians, the subjects of his Midlothian Campaign. As a European statesman he was embarrassed by the situation in Ireland. Schwartzenberg, the Austrian Chancellor, had been quick to point out the deficiencies in British rule in Ireland when Gladstone criticised the treatment of political prisoners in Naples. This was one of the key factors which influenced him in 1868 when he put Ireland at the forefront of his legislative programme. By 1885 it was clear that his policy of religious and agrarian reform had not solved Irish problems and he needed to think in terms of a more radical, long-term response.

Other short-term factors impelled Gladstone towards Home Rule at this time. He was seriously worried by the news of widespread violence and disorder in Ireland and had no confidence in coercion as a long-term solution. He believed that without some degree of self-government there was a real danger of revolution in Ireland. At the same time he always retained that characteristic optimism of Victorian Liberalism and did not believe, as many English politicians did, that the Irish were naturally violent and incapable of ruling themselves. Gladstone was also persuaded by the strength of the Home Rule Party in the House of Commons and a realisation that their numbers were likely to increase following the Third Reform Act. He felt that his government timetable in the early 1880s had been devastated, not only by the Irish Party's obstructionism, but also by the unforeseen Irish legislation. Gladstone was probably convinced of the appropriateness and justice of Home Rule during the cruise he took in August when he visited Norway. He was very impressed by the success this small nation was making of its autonomy while still recognising Sweden as overlord. On 1 November Gladstone received from Katherine O'Shea Parnell's 'proposed Constitution for Ireland'. This was the stimulus for Gladstone to commit to paper his own ideas for a Home Rule Bill. Critics at the time and since have accused Gladstone of using Home Rule to further his ambition, as a means of controlling his party and staying in power. While it is true that his wife and niece urged that he alone understood the Irish question and that he owed it to Cavendish to solve it, they did not necessarily persuade him that he should introduce Home Rule.

Almost as Gladstone was coming to the conclusion that Home Rule was the least measure that would be acceptable to Parnell and his party, he was also reaching another decision: that such a measure would have a greater chance of success if introduced by the Conservative government. There were perfectly valid reasons for believing this. He was mindful of similar legislation passed by Conservative governments (Catholic Emancipation in 1829 and Repeal of the Corn Laws in 1846). He believed, quite rightly, that a bill introduced by a Conservative government was more likely to be passed by the Lords. The Conservative Irish Viceroy, Lord Carnarvon, had already been responsible for the federation of Canada in 1867 and favoured a similar solution for Ireland. Salisbury's government had already shown apparent goodwill towards Ireland in dropping the Coercion Act and passing Lord Ashbourne's Act which allowed tenants to borrow the whole purchase price of their holdings from the government at a preferential rate of interest. So Gladstone advised Parnell, through Katherine O'Shea, to work with the Conservatives. He intimated there would be Liberal support for a Conservative Home Rule Bill.

The general election result of November 1885 which gave 333 seats to the Liberals, 251 to the Conservatives and 86 to the Parnellites did not change Gladstone's mind. Unfortunately, a Conservative measure was never really likely at this time. Though Salisbury shared with Gladstone a Christian devoutness, he tended towards pessimism rather than optimism. He was basically opposed to any extension of political power beyond a relatively narrow elite. He did not believe the Irish were sufficiently responsible to handle any degree of self-government. He was cynical and fatalistic to the extent that he believed the Irish hated the English and there was no political remedy for this. He was no Peelite statesman and he certainly did not understand Gladstone's

Figure 8 Cartoon showing Britannia having to choose between Gladstone (Home Rule) and Salisbury (Perpetual Coercion)

altruism. He thought his suggestion was a ploy to divide the Conservative Party and regain power for himself. In addition, there was little support for Home Rule in the cabinet except from Carnarvon.

The 'Hawarden Kite' signalled the end of this stalemate. Gladstone's youngest son Herbert, himself an MP and an enthusiastic supporter of Home Rule, gave an interview to the National Press Agency which resulted in headlines such as 'HOME RULE. Mr Gladstone's scheme' in the *Pall Mall Gazette*, the leading London evening paper. It was now widely assumed that the Liberals would introduce Home Rule; Parnell began to see the Liberal Party as the better bet; Gladstone received worrying news from the Special Branch in Ireland that there was impending trouble over rents and interest repayments on loans advanced for land purchase. A serious breakdown in law and order seemed imminent. There was also apparently a real danger that the Irish MPs were likely to take matters into their own hands by leaving Westminster and forming their own assembly in Dublin. Gladstone now saw his role clearly: it was his duty to introduce a Home Rule Bill. But he had not prepared his party or the country for this.

At the end of January the Parnellites and Liberals voted together against the government and Salisbury resigned. Despite the Queen's trepidation about 'this half crazy and really in many ways ridiculous old man' she was obliged to ask him to form a third government.

First Home Rule Bill 1886

Gladstone introduced his Government of Ireland Bill on 8 April to a packed House of Commons in a speech lasting three-and-a-half hours – remarkable for the mastery of detail, powerful arguments and compelling delivery. He proposed to modify the Act of Union rather than repeal it by devolving the powers of the Westminster parliament to a legislature in Dublin.

The main terms were:

Government of Ireland Bill 1886

◢ An Irish legislature would be one chamber, composed of two 'orders':

a) 28 Irish peers plus 75 members elected for a term of five years by electors who occupied land to the value of at least £25 per annum;

b) the present 101 Irish MPs plus 101 new ones.

◢ The orders could be required to vote separately and the first could veto the proposals of the second for three years.

◢ No member of the Irish legislature could sit at Westminster.

◢ Responsibility for war and peace, the defence forces, foreign treaties, trade and navigation, customs and excise, coinage, weights and measures, copyright and patents, posts and telegraphs, titles and honours and lighthouses would remain with the Westminster parliament.

◢ Ireland would pay £4,236,000 per annum as her share of imperial expenses and £360,000 as her share of the interest on the national debt. These figures were fixed for 30 years. The figures could only be increased in time of war. At the time it amounted to one-fifteenth of the United Kingdom budget, but it would clearly be a great bargain for the Irish if there was inflation in the future.

◢ The Irish assembly could raise taxes for use within Ireland.

There followed a lengthy and high-quality debate in the Commons during which impressive speeches were made on both sides and there was considerable interest in the country. Gladstone believed further land reform was necessary to bring peace to Ireland and had originally planned to introduce a Land Purchase Bill simultaneously with Home Rule. According to this scheme, the government would buy out the landlords for a sum equal to 20 years' rent and the new owners would pay the State back in annual instalments 20% lower than their present rent. But Gladstone saw no point in alarming the Liberals with land purchase when they were already unsure about Home Rule so the Land Bill was introduced the following month.

Despite Gladstone's great speeches the Government of Ireland Bill was defeated at its second reading on 7 June by 341 votes to 311. The vast majority of the 103 Liberals who failed to support their leader actually voted with the opposition. Gladstone decided to dissolve parliament right away.

Why did Gladstone fail to achieve Home Rule at this time?

Gladstone must bear a large measure of responsibility for the failure of Home Rule at this time. There is a good deal of truth in Lord Randolph Churchill's sneer that he was 'an old man in a hurry'. Like Peel over protection in 1846, Gladstone may justifiably be accused of failing to educate his party, but this time both the country and the party were unprepared: Home Rule had not been mentioned in the Liberal election programme nor in Gladstone's own speeches. On the other hand in 1846 the sustained and effective campaign by the Anti-Corn Law League meant that people were well aware of the issues involved in Repeal of the Corn Laws. It is perhaps understandable that Gladstone should wish to keep his own counsel until after the election for fear of causing divisions in his party, but even after the election Gladstone did not make any great speeches outside the Commons, he wrote no pamphlets, neither did he exploit his links with the press as he had done in his previous crusades for great moral causes.

It is surprising that Gladstone did not make more effort to keep the support of key Liberals. He prepared the Government of Ireland Bill like a budget and the cabinet knew little about it before its sensational publication. There was perhaps little he could have done about Hartington who had already refused to serve in the cabinet and was opposed to any further concessions to the Irish. Not only had he been thwarted in his party leadership ambitions by Gladstone, he had never forgotten the Irish had murdered his brother in Phoenix Park. But Gladstone was right when he wrote to Granville: 'Hartington has displayed much more activity against us than he ever showed on our behalf as friend and colleague.' As far as Chamberlain was concerned Gladstone clearly underestimated the amount of damage he could do to an already weakened party. It was he who made by far the most powerful speeches against Home Rule and he had a large following in the country. Chamberlain was already nursing a grievance because Gladstone had offered him a less senior post in the cabinet than he had expected. He then had to suffer a further snub when Gladstone removed the parliamentary draughtsman working with him on his local government bill and transferred him to the Irish one. Gladstone now had both the leading Radical *and* the leading Whig against him. In the light of the strenuous efforts Gladstone made to maintain John Bright's support in his first government, it seems surprising that he did not do more this time than the two-hour interview recorded in Bright's diary to persuade him of the rightness of his course of action. Bright's letter of opposition to Home Rule, while ostensibly declining to advise others how to vote, was crucial in deciding the outcome of the parliamentary vote.

Once the Government of Ireland Bill had been published, the Conservatives saw their duty clearly as defenders of the union against Irish murderers and cattle maimers. Salisbury made his views plain in a speech in May when he declared that the Irish were as unfit for self-government as the Hottentots (the whites' name for an African tribe) and if public money was to be spent, its best use would be in paying for the emigration of the Irish to Manitoba (Canada). He advocated 20 years of 'resolute government' for Ireland. There was little Gladstone could have done about this but he certainly underestimated the problem of Ulster and was not prepared to make any separate provision for this area.

I cannot conceal the conviction that the voice of Ireland, as a whole, has at this moment clearly and constitutionally spoken ... when five-sixths of its lawfully chosen representatives are of one mind in this matter ... I cannot allow it to be said that a Protestant minority in Ulster or elsewhere is to rule the question at large for Ireland.

Lord Randolph Churchill (who had only recently made overtures to Parnell) now decided, for his own purposes, 'to play the Orange card'. His slogan 'Ulster will fight, Ulster will be right' united all Ulstermen, Liberals and Tories, tenants as well as landowners, against the Bill.

In the country at large there was considerable opposition to Home Rule. Ireland might be regarded with indifference or boredom but towards the Irish themselves there was a feeling of hostility. For many working class people the Irish were immigrant labourers who took their jobs by accepting lower pay, for others they were the murderers of Phoenix Park and the perpetrators of dynamite outrages in London. There was a good deal of anti-Catholic prejudice and the Irish were widely regarded as ignorant and superstitious. While supporters of Home Rule saw it as a benefit to remove the unruly and subversive Irish MPs from Westminster, others thought it would be the first step towards an inevitable separation and independence. John Bright reflected the view of many when he wrote of Gladstone: 'I thought he placed far too much confidence in the leaders of the Rebel Party. I could place none in them, and the general feeling was and is that any terms made with them would not be kept, and that, thro' them, I could not hope for reconciliation with discontented and disloyal Ireland.' Many Radicals objected to the cost of the Land Purchase scheme to the neglect of social welfare reforms at home. Intellectuals and influential leaders of Liberal opinion such as A. V. Dicey, Leslie Stephen and Matthew Arnold were alienated by what they saw as Gladstone's dictatorial leadership and surrender to a violent and vocal minority.

There is no doubt that by this time Gladstone had become somewhat detached from his party and that he underestimated the difficulties in getting Home Rule on to the statute book. Perhaps with more careful preparation, he might have kept the support of more of his party, but he was never a party manager; he saw himself more as a national statesman in the mould of his mentor, Peel, and like him, he broke his party.

Answering documents questions

This is an important skill, as documents questions can account for a high proportion of the marks on the exam paper. In some ways they appear to be easier than essay questions because they are broken down into five or six sub-questions.

Each sub-question is targeted at a different objective. You need to identify that target correctly and answer in a relevant way, so as not to waste time on comments which cannot score. The most common types of questions are:

1 *Recall of knowledge* These come first and carry few marks. Answer *briefly*.

2 *Reliability* You need to ask yourself some questions, for example:
How much fact does the source contain and how much opinion?
Are the facts accurate as far as you know?
Are the opinions likely to be well informed?
What do you know about the person writing?
Has the date any bearing?
Is the type of source (e.g. diary, letter, speech) significant?
Can you detect the purpose behind the source?
Is there a particular tone to it?
Does the use of language tell you anything?
Remember the issue of reliability is about whether the source provides a sound basis for drawing conclusions, making judgements, testing hypotheses, evaluating other sources.

3 *Tone or language* You need to distinguish these:
TONE means the overall effect conveyed by the source in terms of the attitudes, emotions, feelings of the writer/speaker.
LANGUAGE refers to the specific words/phrases used by the writer/speaker to convey the tone.
Look out for examples of the following: fear, anger, excitement, sarcasm, hope, cynicism, etc.

4 *Sufficiency* This type of question usually comes last and carries most marks. Look carefully through each source for information. Then from your own knowledge, think of *other* aspects which are *not* covered in the sources. The two parts of the question will not necessarily be

balanced. Most of the information might be in the sources, or they might be seriously inadequate, but you must make some points from the sources and some from your own knowledge.

The First Irish Home Rule Bill

Study Documents I, II and III below, and then answer questions (a) to (f) which follow:

DOCUMENT I

20 March 1886. Downing Street. Long <u>interview for two hours with Mr Gladstone at his request</u>. He explained <u>much of his policy</u> as to a Dublin Parl[iamen]t and as to <u>Land Purchase</u>. I objected to the Land Policy as unnecessary . . . As to a Dublin Parlt, I argued that he was
5   making a surrender all along the line. A Dublin Parlt would work with constant friction, and would press against any barrier he might create to keep up the unity of the three Kingdoms . . .
Mr G is in favour of excluding all Irish representation from the Imperial Parlt. Thinks Irish members in Dublin and at Westminster not possible.
10 Irish members think they could not supply representatives for both Houses.
I told him I thought to get rid of the Irishmen from Westminster, such as we have known them for five or six years past, would do something to make his propositions less offensive and distasteful to Gt Britain, tho' it
15 tends to more complete separation . . .
I thought he placed far too much confidence in the leaders of the rebel party. I could place none in them, and the general feeling was and is that any terms made with them would not be kept, and that, thro' them, I could not hope for reconciliation with discontented and disloyal Ireland.
(*The Diaries of John Bright*)

DOCUMENT II

20 I decided some time ago, that if <u>the GOM</u> went for Home Rule, <u>the Orange card</u> would be the one to play. Please God may it turn out the ace of trumps and not the two . . . It may be that this dark cloud which is now impending over Ireland, will pass away without breaking. If it does, I believe you and your descendants will be safe for a long time to come.
25 Her Majesty's Government hesitates. Like Macbeth before the murder of Duncan, Mr Gladstone asks for time. Before he plunges the knife into the heart of the British Empire he reflects he hesitates . . . The <u>Loyalists of Ulster</u> should wait and watch; organise and prepare. Diligence and vigilance ought to be your watchword; so that the blow, if it does come,

30 may not come upon you as a thief in the night and may not find you
unready and taken by surprise ...
(*Lord R. Churchill to Fitzgibbon, 16 February 1886*)

DOCUMENT III
In America or Switzerland federalism has developed because existing
states wished to be combined into some kind of national unity.
Federalism in England would necessarily mean the breaking up of a
35 nation in order to form a body of states ...
The vast majority of the United Kingdom, including a million or more of
the inhabitants of Ireland, have expressed their will to maintain the
Union. Popular government means government in accordance with the
will of the majority, and therefore according to the principles of popular
40 government the majority of the United Kingdom have a right to maintain
the Union. Their wish is decisive, and ought to terminate the whole
agitation in favour of Home Rule.
(A. V. Dicey, *England's case against Home Rule*, 1886)

(Maximum marks)

(a) In the context of these Documents, explain the
meaning of:
  (i) 'Land Purchase' (line 3);
  (ii) 'the GOM' (line 20); and
  (iii) 'the Orange card' (line 21). (3)
(b) From your knowledge of the context, explain the
circumstances in which John Bright had his
'interview for two hours with Mr Gladstone at his
request' (line 1). Why might Gladstone have been so
anxious to explain to Bright 'much of his policy'
(line 2)? (4)
(c) What does Document I reveal of Bright's attitude
towards the Irish Question? (5)
(d) How does the language used by Churchill in
Document II (lines 20–31) enhance the force of his
message to the 'Loyalists of Ulster' (line 27)? (4)
(e) Evaluate the case against Home Rule presented in
Document III (lines 32–42) (4)
(f) How fully do these Documents illustrate the situation
created in British politics by Gladstone's
announcement of his adoption of Home Rule in
1886? (5)

ULEAC 1990

CHAPTER SIX

GLADSTONE'S LEGACY

Objective

◢ To analyse Gladstone's legacy to his party and country in the short and longer terms.

The broken party

Gladstone's immediate and most obvious legacy was a divided Liberal Party. The 1886 general election provided dramatic evidence of this. The Conservatives won 316 seats and the Liberals were reduced to 196, giving a majority of about 100 to the opponents of Home Rule if the Liberal Unionists were to vote with the Conservatives (though this was by no means certain for other issues). Yet the success of the Liberal Unionists gives a misleading impression of the unpopularity of Home Rule at this time for 73 of them won because the Conservative candidate stood down in their constituencies. It was difficult to acquire and promote a new Gladstonian Liberal candidate in so short a time and the Unionist candidate gained some two-thirds of the Conservative vote. In constituencies where there was a straight contest between Liberal and Conservative, the Liberal vote often increased and some seats were even regained. The anti-Home Rule feeling had been strongly encouraged by the press which, from being strongly Liberal, swung to Unionism far more firmly than the electorate.

There is ample evidence to substantiate the view that Home Rule merely accelerated divisions in the Liberal Party which already existed. There had already been important Whig defections during the 1880–85 ministry, such as the Dukes of Argyll and Bedford and the Marquis of Lansdowne. Aristocrats and landowners had become increasingly dismayed both by Liberal legislation which endangered their interests and radical programmes which threatened to do so. The majority of the 94 Liberals who voted against Gladstone in 1886 had aristocratic or landed connections, though almost 30% did not.

There were other groups among the Liberal Right who were becoming disillusioned with both party and leader before this time. There were manufacturers and businessmen concerned about the Employers' Liability Act of 1880 and the Second Irish Land Act of 1881 which, in their view, marked unwarranted government interference in the principles of free contract and there were intellectuals who thought Gladstone was betraying the traditional Liberal principles of individual freedom. In 1885 Dicey wrote:

The whole theory of modern Liberals is that the State is to take in hand the control of the masses, and override the rights of individuals ... Commonsense tells me that there is less practical risk of individual liberty being seriously endangered under a Conservative than under a Liberal administration ... Once you desert the solid ground of individual freedom, you can find no resting place till you reach the abyss of Socialism.

After 1886 Dicey was to be the most passionate advocate of Unionism outside parliament. But others were leaving the Liberal Party because of its failure to go far enough down the socialist road. William Morris campaigned hard for the Liberals in the 1880 election but left in 1881 in protest at the Irish Coercion Act and the government's failure to enact social reform. Two years later a group of disenchanted advanced Liberals, led by Sidney and Beatrice Webb, began to set up the *Fabian Society*.

KEY TERM

The **Fabian Society** was formally founded in 1884 by Sidney and Beatrice Webb and George Bernard Shaw to promote the establishment of a democratic socialist society. It was named after a Roman general, Fabius Cunctator who defeated Hannibal by delaying and avoiding direct confrontation. Fabians sought, and still do seek, to promote socialism gradually, by publishing pamphlets and organising debates. It was particularly influential between 1900 and 1914 in shaping the ideals of the emerging Labour Party and as a source of ideas for the Liberal government's social reforms.

In the Commons the leading representative of these views was Joseph Chamberlain but he had his own reasons for deserting the Liberals over Home Rule. When he resigned in March 1886 it was over the proposed exclusion of Irish MPs from Westminster, but he was bitter that his own plan for local government in Ireland had been rejected. He saw his move as a step towards ultimate party leadership as he intimated in a letter to his brother:

I cannot, of course, work with the Tories, and Hartington is quite as much hostile to my radical views as to W. G.'s Irish plans. But in time the situation will clear. Either Mr Gladstone will succeed and get the Irish question out of the way, or he will fail. In either case he will retire from politics and I do not suppose the Liberal Party will accept Childers or even John Morley as its permanent leader.

Chamberlain's plans were confounded by Gladstone's refusal to resign. The only notion that Chamberlain had in common with Hartington was a shared belief in the weakness and unpatriotic nature of Gladstone's foreign policy. At the same time it was Chamberlain's imperialist views which meant he could never be leader of the Radicals because they were so out of step with most Radical opinion which agreed with Gladstone on foreign policy. Thus the majority of Radicals chose to stay with Gladstone in 1886.

The fate of Home Rule

Gladstone did not abandon Home Rule in 1886. On the contrary its rejection in the Commons clarified his future: it was his duty to solve the Irish Question and to do so he must continue as leader of the Liberal Party. He judged that the speedy introduction of Home Rule was the only way to keep Ireland within the United Kingdom. In opposition he set out to educate both the Party and the country accordingly and, despite failing eyesight and increasing deafness, he wrote articles (e.g. 'Home Rule for Ireland. An appeal to the Tory Householder') and again made speeches to large audiences. He sought to show that Home Rule was not a sudden change of policy but fitted in with Britain's well-established colonial policy, that it had been shown to work well on the continent of Europe, and that it would be the final step in the settlement of Ireland and not the first of many leading to independence. By 1890 Gladstone's plan seemed to be working and the Liberals had won 12 seats from the Conservatives at by-elections.

Although Gladstone hoped to win an outright Liberal majority sufficiently large that the Lords would not dare to reject a Home Rule bill, his strategy also depended for its success on a close working alliance with Parnell and his Irish Party. To this end Gladstone now held direct discussions with Parnell and in December 1889 Parnell was an overnight guest at Hawarden. In his diary Gladstone recorded: 'He is certainly one of the very best people to deal with that I have ever known ... He seems to notice and appreciate everything.' This may have been true at the time but Gladstone overestimated Parnell's political leadership. Following the divorce case brought by Katherine O'Shea's husband, naming Parnell as co-respondent, and which he refused to contest, Parnell became a source of division and bitterness in the Home Rule movement in both countries. Gladstone knew that the success of Home Rule depended on strength and unity. The Liberal Party could not afford to lose the support of the Nonconformists whose vociferous moralising was crucial in persuading him that Parnell could not remain as leader of the Irish Party:

... the dominant question, now properly before Mr Parnell for his consideration, is what is the best course for him to adopt with a view to the furtherance of the interests of Home Rule in Great Britain. And with deep pain but without any doubt, I judge that those interests require his retirement at the present time from his leadership.

Had Parnell taken Gladstone's advice his own tragedy need not have been also a tragedy for his cause. At the end of 1890 even Gladstone's customary optimism was dimmed.

The 1892 election brought the Liberals a disappointing majority of only four over the Conservatives, but there were 81 Irish MPs and only 46 Liberal Unionists. So began Gladstone's fourth ministry, though he confided to his diary: 'Frankly: for the condition (now) of my senses, I am no longer fit for public life: yet bidden to walk in it.' Nevertheless he launched his second Government of Ireland Bill in February 1893. He steered it through all its stages in the Commons himself, making 80 speeches in all, sometimes four in a day and all of them spontaneous for he would not have been able to see any notes had he made them. This was an extraordinary feat of stamina for any premier, let alone one over 80. The Bill passed its Third Reading in the Commons by 34 votes, but a week later was thrown out of the Lords by a remarkable 419 votes to 41, the largest majority ever recorded with 82% of those entitled to vote doing so. Gladstone might still have been prepared to dissolve parliament on the issue of the Lords thwarting the will of the elected chamber, but there was no support for this among his colleagues. Indeed many already begrudged the time taken by the Irish bill and wanted to return to domestic reform and the Newcastle programme which Gladstone had endorsed during the election campaign.

This failure to legislate for the working class was to be as important for the future of the Liberal Party as the schism. Although Gladstone had made his reputation as 'the People's William', he was both detached from and unsympathetic to the emerging working-class politics at the end of the century. Many newly enfranchised working class people who had voted for Gladstone's Liberal Party felt betrayed by his subsequent concentration on Home Rule and lack of social reform. Agricultural labourers were disappointed that there had been no improvement in their living conditions. Working-class men joined the new trade unions which were more political and saw organised industrial action (like the gas workers' and dockers' strikes of 1889) as the means to improvement rather than the Liberal ideas of self-help. Liberal failure to recognise working-class aspirations and neglect of their interests left a vacuum into which the Labour Party would step. The view claiming that had Gladstone been able to carry a successful Home Rule measure then the way would have been cleared for social welfare, and the Liberal Party would have become the party of social reform, neglects Gladstone's distinct lack of enthusiasm for such reform. Though he adopted the proposals of the party conference at Newcastle in 1891 for a wide range of reforms such as an end to plural voting, triennial parliaments, payment of MPs, restrictions on the hours of work, employers' liability in industrial accidents, death duties and the establishment of district and parish councils, he did so as the price of Home Rule. He did not refer to the Newcastle programme in his election speeches.

Once the Liberal Unionists had decamped, the Liberals who remained were more united than they had been at any time since Gladstone's first ministry, but when he finally resigned in 1894 he left the party weaker in the sense that he left no obvious successor. The party was also financially weaker. In 1889 Gladstone told the National Liberal Federation 'the wealthy and powerful had been gradually detaching themselves from the body of the Liberal Party and finding their most natural associations in Toryism'. Many of the party's wealthiest supporters had left in 1886. The party seemed ill placed to win elections.

The survival of Liberal ideas

Although Gladstonian Liberalism seemed to be a nineteenth-century phenomenon whose ideas were inappropriate for the twentieth century, many of Gladstone's ideas have proved surprisingly durable. The great Liberal landslide of 1906 was won very much on traditional Liberal ideas such as free trade, and the condemnation of the crimes of British Imperialism (in the Boer War); the support of Nonconformists was regained by opposition to the 1904 Licensing Act (the 'brewers' Bill'); and many of its measures in office were reminiscent of the last Gladstone government: Home Rule, death duties, education, land reform, plural voting, reducing the powers of the Lords. Many Liberals saw the First World War as the awful conclusion to Gladstone's grim warnings of the results of militarism and imperialism and of course Britain entered the war on the typically Gladstonian principle of preserving the neutrality and independence of the small state of Belgium.

In post-war Britain Lord Rosebery's premonition of the 'elimination of Liberalism, leaving the two forces of Socialism and Reaction to face each other' seemed to be coming true and the principles of Victorian Liberalism appeared more and more anachronistic. In the years of consensus politics after the Second World War, with the State increasingly involved in every aspect of people's lives, public spending and State intervention were seen as virtues. At the end of the twentieth century, however, there has been a revival of interest in and support for a number of Gladstone's ideas. Thatcher hijacked some in the 1980s: minimal direct taxation, public economy and free market economics were presented as ideals, though not, of course, Gladstone's principles of foreign policy. Since then there has been a widespread questioning of the role of the State as the best provider of welfare and social benefits of all kinds and genuine concern about the cost of State provision together with an encouragement to individuals to provide for themselves. Gladstone's Government of Ireland Bill remains a blueprint for current devolution plans for Scotland and the European Union is surely the logical outcome of Gladstone's Concert of Europe ideas.

A new style of politics

There are many aspects of present-day politics which we owe to Gladstone. He was the first politician to address the public directly. The Midlothian Campaign was a new style of electioneering. It was not a campaign to win a small parliamentary constituency, more one to re-establish his pre-eminence as the leading politician of the day, to enthuse the population with Liberal ideas and to make a direct appeal to voters nationwide. Although Gladstone calculated he addressed 86,930 people during the Campaign, his intended audience was much larger than this. It included the newspaper-reading public. Gladstone was the first politician deliberately and systematically to use the press to promote his party, his policies and his own career. He was the first media politician. Though he had at his disposal fewer resources than today, he would surely have used the radio and television to great advantage had they been available to him. He was the first European politician whose recorded voice was heard across the English-speaking world, from the United States to Australia, via Edison's phonograph.

Gladstone began the personalisation of politics. He greatly enhanced the role of party leader and began the convention of the party leader addressing the annual party conference. He was the first to have his wife regularly on the political platform beside him and, in her seventies, Catherine was invited to be the first president of the Women's Liberal Federation. Under Gladstone's leadership the political rally was born, essential to the vitality of the party. Whether as 'the People's William' or the GOM there were few Liberal households in the 1870s and 1880s where Gladstone's portrait was not displayed above the mantelpiece or painted on a jug or on a plate. Even Tories had his portrait – on the inside of chamber pots. In a typically sneering speech in 1884 Lord Randolph Churchill said:

The Prime Minister is the greatest living master of the art of personal political advertisement ... Every act of his, whether it be for the purposes of health, or of recreation, or of religious devotion, is spread before the eyes of every man, woman and child in the United Kingdom on large and glaring placards. For the purpose of an autumn holiday a large transatlantic steamer is specially engaged, the Poet Laureate

adorns the suite and receives a peerage as his reward, and the incidents of the voyage
are luncheon with the Emperor of Russia and tea with the Queen of Denmark.

Despite the sarcasm, there was more than a grain of truth in these comments. Queen Victoria was particularly incensed that Gladstone and his family seemed to be usurping her role as first family of the nation. In 1877 Catherine opened the grounds of Hawarden to the public: thousands of admiring day-trippers from the Lancashire cotton towns came to see Gladstone fell a tree and to take away some of the wood shavings.

Much of the structure of our political system as we know it today was established by Gladstone, either during his premierships or his time as Chancellor of the Exchequer. Traditionally, the second job in the cabinet had been that of Foreign Secretary. Gladstone elevated the position of Chancellor until it became second only to that of Prime Minister. He drew up his own legislative programme and acted independently without consulting other government departments. In 1861, to avoid rejection by the Lords of any one part, Gladstone brought all his financial measures together in a single bill and so began the annual budget. Also in 1861 he set up the Public Accounts Committee which still has a central role in the Commons' scrutiny of government expenditure. In 1866 he was responsible for the Exchequer and Audit Act which completed the Commons' control over expenditure as well as taxation. It created the office of Comptroller and Auditor General which still exists today, though he now has a staff of 900 which would have greatly shocked Gladstone! In his role as Leader of the House of Commons, which Gladstone combined with First Lord of the Treasury, he streamlined parliamentary procedures with the introduction of the Guillotine and the Closure. In 1881 he suggested to the Speaker that all questions to the Prime Minister be put together in batches rather than being interspersed at random amongst others. This was the beginning of Prime Minister's Question Time as we know it today. Under Gladstone the parliamentary year became longer. When he first became an MP parliament rose in August for the shooting season and did not return until February.

It was due to the legislation of Gladstone's governments that elections became recognisably modern. There was the Ballot Act of course, but possibly more important at the time was the Corrupt and Illegal Practices Act of 1883, which forms the basis of our electoral law today. By setting maximum limits for election expenses in a constituency according to the number of voters it did much to restrict corruption. By this time five-sixths of the parliamentary seats were contested, unlike the beginning of Gladstone's career when only a tiny minority were contested. The two-party system was established more firmly, partly as a result of Gladstone's rivalry with Disraeli. After 1886 the Irish Nationalists were tied to the Liberals and Gladstone's remaining as party leader gave Chamberlain time to learn to work with Salisbury. Though he had intended his break with the Liberals to be temporary, he and other Unionists joined the Conservatives in 1895.

Apart from politics there are many aspects of life today which are attributable to Gladstone. The Bank Holiday Act of his first ministry established fixed public holidays, initially for office workers, on Boxing Day, Easter Monday and Whit Monday. The Post Office Savings Bank which Gladstone created in 1861 for small savers still exists. In 1871, in the interests of economy, Gladstone launched the halfpenny post-card. Little did he realise that, by the end of the century, it would have led to the mass practice of sending picture postcards – a custom more popular than ever for holidaymakers at the end of the twentieth century.

It is virtually impossible to summarise Gladstone and his career, so complex was his personality, so many and varied his interests and so long his public life. He was more than just a great Prime Minister: had his career ended in 1868, he would still have been a figure of national importance. Though not a party leader in the modern sense, he held together the many diverse groups within the Victorian Liberal Party and provided it with a philosophy. If his last years were disappointing and added little to his reputation, he nevertheless remains the dominant figure of the nineteenth century who set the political agenda for a great deal of that time.

FURTHER READING

There is an enormous amount of published material on Gladstone.

A serious student should at least dip into Roy Jenkins' prize winning biography *Gladstone* (Macmillan, 1995), which is beautifully written and full of interesting insights.

The best single volume life is still E. J. Feuchtwanger's *Gladstone* (Penguin, 1975).

The editor of his diaries, H. C. G. Matthew, is the acknowledged authority on Gladstone. His introductions to the diaries are published in two volumes, *Gladstone 1909–1874*, and *Gladstone 1875–1898* (OUP, 1986 and 1995) but most A-level students are likely to find these too difficult and detailed for their purposes.

There is a clear commentary on the political history covered here in T. A. Jenkins. *The Liberal Ascendancy 1830–1886* (Macmillan, 1994). Some interesting ideas about Gladstone's relationship with his party can be found in the Lancaster Pamphlet, Michael Winstanley *Gladstone and the Liberal Party* (Routledge, 1990).

There was no space here to consider the rivalry between Gladstone and Disraeli but students will find interesting comparisons in T. A. Jenkins *Disraeli and Victorian Conservatism* (Macmillan, 1996).

The best biographies of Parnell are F. S. L. Lyons *Charles Stewart Parnell* (Collins, 1977) and Robert Kee *The Laurel and the Ivy* (H. Hamilton, 1994). There are articles on Gladstone, Parnell and Ireland reprinted from *The Modern History Review* in *Britain 1867–1918*, edited by Peter Caterall (Heinemann, 1994).

Shelia Fletcher's *Victorian Girls: Lord Lyttleton's Daughters* (Hambledon Press, 1997) gives a fascinating background about Gladstone's family life and the position of women in Victorian times.

Gladstone's voice can be heard on the tape of *Great Political Speeches* compiled by Peter Hill (BBC/Hodder Audio, 1996).

INDEX

KEY TERMS

Benthamite   54
Dis-establishment   46
Fabian Society   118
Guillotine   103
Suzerainty   90

PROFILES

Aberdeen, Earl of   23
Cardwell, Edward   61
Churchill, Lord Randolph   105
Clarendon, Earl of   61
Cobden, Richard   25
Derby, Earl of   29
Forster, William Edward   41
Granville, Earl of   45
Hartington, Marquis of   45
Huskisson, William   25
Lowe, Robert   61
Ripon, Earl of   25
Russell, Lord John   41
Selborne, Earl of   65

MAIN INDEX

Aberdeen, Lord   23, 28, 33, 40, 80
Afghanistan   87–90
Army reforms   63–5

Beaconsfieldism   14, 85, 101
Bright, John   13, 19, 27, 33, 34–5, 40,
   46, 55–8, 60–1, 71–2, 80–1, 83, 93,
   100, 102, 112–3
Budgets   32–3, 37–8, 72, 124

Canning, George   3, 4, 21, 83
Cardwell, Edward   60–1, 63–5
Chamberlain, Joseph   19, 48, 102,
   111, 118–9
China   24, 78, 80
Churchill, Lord R.   105, 111–2, 123–4
Clarendon, Earl of   44, 60, 61, 63, 101
Cobden, Richard   9, 25–7, 33, 36, 40,
   54, 67, 80–1
Corn Laws   8, 9, 25–6, 27, 111
Crimean War   80–1, 85

Derby, Lord   14, 29–31, 34–3, 43
Disraeli, Benjamin   9, 13, 14, 15, 19,
   31, 34, 39, 43, 71, 73–4, 77, 84–7,
   89–90, 105, 126

Education   66–9, 73
Egypt   90–3

Fenians   96–7, 100–1
Forster, W. E.   40–1, 61, 67, 102, 104

Granville, Earl   14, 15, 44–5, 60, 63,
   84, 91, 111

Hartington, Marquis of   14, 15, 44–5,
   60, 91, 100, 104, 111, 110
Huskisson, William   24–5

Law reform   65–6
Lowe, Robert   50, 60–1, 67, 71

Mill, J. S.   51–2, 55

Newspapers   38–40, 72–3, 109, 123
Nonconformists   8, 47–8, 54, 62,
   67–9, 93, 97, 120

Palmerston, Lord   12, 15, 20, 28, 30,
   34–6, 41, 43, 78–80, 83–4, 90
Parnell, Charles   48, 101–5, 107, 109,
   119–20
Peel, Robert/Peelites   4, 8, 9–12, 15,
   20, 21–6, 29–31, 33–4, 80, 96, 113

Radicals   8, 12, 37, 44, 46–7, 53–5, 62,
   71, 83, 93, 97, 113, 119
Reform Acts   5, 17, 44, 106
Russell, Lord John   12, 15, 30, 33,
   40–1, 43, 97
Russia   74, 80–1, 85–7, 89

Salisbury, Lord   105, 107–9, 112
Selborne, Lord   65
Sudan   91–3

Trade unions   70, 73, 121
Turkey   80–2, 85–7

Victoria, Queen   15–6, 20, 30, 64, 93,
   124

Working class   3, 13, 50–1, 121

Longman History in Depth
Series editor: Christopher Culpin

Titles in the series
Hitler and Nazism (0 582 29736 2)
Causes of the Second World War (0 582 29650 1)
Stalin and the Soviet Union (0 582 29733 8)
Origins of the First World War (0 582 29522 X)
The Russian Revolution (0 582 29731 1)
Parnell and the Irish Question (0 582 29628 5)
Gladstone (0 582 29521 1)
Chartism (0 582 29735 4)
Oliver Cromwell (0 582 29734 6)
Charles I (0 582 29732 X)
Henry VII (0 582 29691 9)

Pearson Education Limited
Edinburgh Gate, Harlow,
Essex, CM20 2JE, England
and Associated Companies throughout the world.

The right of Patricia Tweedie to be identified as the author of this Work has been asserted by her in accordance with the Copyright, Designs and Patents Act of 1988.

First published 1998
© Addison Wesley Longman Limited 1998
Second impression 2002

Set in 9.5/13pt Stone Serif
Printed in Singapore (KHL)

ISBN 0 582 29521 1

Acknowledgements

We are grateful to the following for permission to reproduce photographs:

Courtesy of Mr. C. A. Gladstone, page 7; Mary Evans Picture Library, pages 19 centre, 20 top; Fotomas Index, page 19 bottom; Hulton Deutsch Collection, pages 5, 10; Hulton Getty Collection, page 19 top; Popperfoto, page 20 bottom; Topham Picturepoint, pages 13, 20 centre.

We were unable to trace the copyright holder of the following and would be grateful for any information that would enable us to do so, page 108.

Cover: engraving of Gladstone by W. Biscombe Gardner from a photograph by Samuel A. Walker. Hulton Getty Collection

We are grateful to EDEXCEL Foundation, London Examinations for permission to reproduce an extract and questions from 'The First Irish Home Rule Bill' in London GCE A Level paper 1990.

The publisher's policy is to use paper manufactured from sustainable forests.